Praise for

Free Me from Me

"Ryan Wekenman is a trusted voice for anyone hoping to deepen their self-awareness, pursue emotional and spiritual growth, and become a stronger person of faith."

—Annie F. Downs, *New York Times* bestselling author of *That Sounds Fun*

"You need to read this book! Ryan Wekenman has a crazy ability to explain complex theological topics in simple and practical ways. In a world full of opinions about who you are, *Free Me from Me* is going to help you understand who God says you are and experience the amazing freedom that comes with living a God-centered life!"

—Shawn Johnson, pastor and bestselling author of *Kiss the Fire* and *Attacking Anxiety*

"*Free Me from Me* is a gift. Ryan Wekenman confronts our culture's hyper-fixation on the self and gently restores God to the center—where peace actually becomes possible. For the sake of sanity, please read this book."

—Kory Miller, Christian music artist, songwriter, and worship leader at Red Rocks Church

"*Free Me from Me* is not written for the faint of heart. It is courageous in its transparency and asks as much from the reader. Ryan Wekenman's profound vulnerability invites—perhaps even insists upon—the kind of bravery that true transformation requires: the humility to be lovingly decentered, and the courage to imagine the grace and emerging glory of a life freed from the exhausting burden of self."

—Jeffrey Tacklind, author of
The Winding Path of Transformation and
pastor of Little Church by the Sea, Laguna Beach

Free Me from Me

Free Me from Me

Escaping the Maze of Self-Centeredness by Embracing a God-Centered Life

Ryan Wekenman

WaterBrook

WaterBrook
An imprint of the Penguin Random House Christian Publishing Group, a division of Penguin Random House LLC
1745 Broadway, New York, NY 10019
waterbrookmultnomah.com
penguinrandomhouse.com

Italics in Scripture quotations reflect the author's added emphasis.

Library of Congress Cataloging-in-Publication Data
Names: Wekenman, Ryan author
Title: Free me from me / Ryan Wekenman.
Description: First edition. | New York, NY: WaterBrook, 2026 |
Includes bibliographical references.
Identifiers: LCCN 2025040272 | ISBN 9780593600962 hardcover |
ISBN 9780593600979 ebook
Subjects: LCSH: Christian life | Self—Religious aspects—Christianity |
Peace—Religious aspects—Christianity
Classification: LCC BV4501.3 .W4226 2026
LC record available at https://lccn.loc.gov/2025040272

Printed in the United States of America

1st Printing

First Edition

The authorized representative in the EU for product safety and compliance is Penguin Random House Ireland, Morrison Chambers, 32 Nassau Street, Dublin D02 YH68, Ireland. https://eu-contact.penguin.ie

BOOKMAKING TEAM: Production editor: Jocelyn Kiker • Managing editor: Julia Wallace • Production manager: Katie Zilberman • Copy editor: Kayla Fenstermaker • Proofreaders: Debbie Anderson, Julia Henderson

Book design by Diane Hobbing based on a design by Virginia Norey

For details on special quantity discounts for bulk purchases, contact specialmarketscms@penguinrandomhouse.com.

This book is dedicated to

Me

(Wait, no—I already messed it up. Umm, I guess this book is dedicated to everyone other than me.)

Contents

Free Me from Me

Preface

Lord, Free Me from Me

This book is about one word and a prayer.

The word is *self*—which means this book is about you.

But before we talk about you, let's talk about me.

From the moment I woke up today, I haven't stopped thinking about *me.*

Most of my thoughts have been about me.
All of my prayers have been for me.
Even when I helped someone else, I was trying to make myself feel better.

Hello, my name is Ryan Wekenman, and I'm addicted to me.

Maybe you can relate.

Or maybe you are holier than me.
Better than me.
More sanctified.

Good for you. Don't buy this book; save yourself a couple of bucks. You'll probably end up donating the money to some good cause or something anyway.

As for the rest of us, let's be really honest about a very peculiar challenge the modern world is throwing at us. We live in a world that is obsessed with the self. Every time you scroll through social media, watch the news, or walk out your front door, you are inundated with a message: *It all starts with self.*

Self-help quotes.
Self-improvement books.
Self-discovery assessments.
Self-actualization podcasts.
Self-esteem seminars.
Self-love coaches.

Each a slightly different attempt to figure out what's missing in our lives while starting with the self. Promising answers but then leaving us with more questions. Because here's the thing (brace yourself—are you ready?): This earth and everything on it was here long before you were.

You didn't create you.
You didn't create this world.
You definitely didn't create this universe.

God did that. Everything starts with God. And spirituality is supposed to be a humble reminder that you are part of this bigger story he is writing. But the dominant narrative in our culture today takes God out of the center and replaces him with self. Where living *your truth* becomes more important than discovering *the Truth.* You are bombarded with that message everywhere, so it can be easy to fall back (intentionally or unintentionally) into the trap of believing it all revolves around you.

When self-centeredness gets its hands on spirituality . . .

God's image becomes self-image.
God's righteousness becomes self-righteousness.

God's help becomes self-help.
Soul care becomes self-care.

And as good and open-minded as it sounds at first, when you start with the self, you end up with an impossibly heavy weight on your shoulders you were never created to carry. This takes many forms:

Maybe it's the pressure to be morally good. At some level, you believe that the blessings in your life are tied to your good behavior, so you've turned spirituality into a performance you're waiting to be judged on. Which is only good news on good days. And there are a lot of bad days. So all the pressure has you feeling weary and burdened.

Or maybe it's the pressure to have all the answers. As if a few decades is long enough to figure out an infinite God. You live with this low-grade anxiety that someone will ask you a question and you won't know the answer. So all the pressure has you feeling weary and burdened.

Maybe you picked up this book as your next self-help resource. Hoping to add a few more mantras to your self-improvement tool belt. But if you're being honest, even with all the work and all the self-talk, you still feel like something is wrong. Except with the added pressure of knowing you've tried everything and are still missing the mark.

Or maybe you're part of a growing number of people trying to add new age practices to your journey—spirit guides, tarot cards, astrology, psychedelics. That attractive influencer who is really good at explaining things claimed they were going to enhance your spiritual journey, but they overpromised and underdelivered. And now you're confused about what the practices are and why they seem like such a good idea but leave you feeling weary and burdened.

All these hypotheticals have one thing in common—you. They are examples of a lifestyle and "spirituality" that put the self at the center. And when you do that, the result, every time, will be the unrelenting pressure of carrying a weight you were never created to carry—one that throws you into a maze of self-centeredness.

And so, this book. The premise is simple:

Living with the self at the center creates pressure.
Living with Christ at the center brings rest for the soul.*

But here's the thing: It makes total sense that we try to start with the self. After all, you are you. You were thrown into this whole existence thing without anyone briefing you on it beforehand. You just showed up and started trying to figure it all out.

So before you roll your eyes and throw this book across the room, let me be clear: I think you're awesome. Seriously. I do.

You matter more than you realize.
You are more significant than you know.

This isn't a book about bashing self—a two-hundred-something-page tome about how awful you are. It's the opposite. It's a deep dive into the immense potential waiting to be unlocked in you, once you get the order right, as a human created in the image of God.

* I will use *God-centered spirituality* and *Christ-centered spirituality* interchangeably throughout this book simply because the triune God is one in essence and three in person. While a deep dive into the roles of the Father, Son, and Holy Spirit is an incredibly important conversation, it's not the focus of this book.

Which takes us to the prayer this book is about. A prayer we will pray a thousand times on our journey together. A short prayer with the power to change everything about your life:

Lord, free me from me.

In a world obsessed with the self, this prayer will set you free, but first, it will take you on a journey that is not for the faint of heart. With this prayer as our tour guide, we will explore the theological, psychological, and cultural reasons it's becoming increasingly difficult to see beyond ourselves.

Two thousand years ago, Jesus gave us this invitation: "Come to me, all you who are weary and burdened, and I will give you rest."[1] Note, the prerequisite for the rest is to go to him, taking self out of the center. We like to skip that part but still wonder why we're burned out.

My hope is that this book will feel like a deep exhale for the tired soul. By the end of it, I believe you will discover the immense freedom found in putting God back at the center of the story. Where you . . .

Stop overthinking every awkward social interaction.
Stop worrying you aren't doing enough.
Stop making everything about you.

In short, you will notice how much pressure you've been putting on maintaining your self-image and trade that in for the freedom of being made in God's image.

So if you've noticed yourself becoming exhausted with *trying* on your own to be the best friend, co-worker, spouse, leader, parent, [insert other label here], keep reading and find out how Jesus's command "Come to me" is actually good news for every aspect of your life. Maybe you don't need to be in therapy forever or quit your job or take a hundred self-care days this year. Maybe you just need Jesus.

Along the way, you may rediscover the gift all those other things can be when you stop putting so much pressure on them to save you.

And so, Lord, free us from us.

Introduction

From Self-Centered to God-Centered

"Fully in . . . letting go."[1]

The voice belonged to Wim Hof. A wild Dutch man who had been running barefoot in the Arctic, plunging into freezing water, and taking the self-help scene by storm.

I was all in on the different methods.

Workouts.
Ice baths.
Breath work.
Grounding.

On April 19, 2020, I was combining all four, squeezing the ice bath in during the second round of breath work right after a difficult workout.[*] *If a little self-help helps,* my mind reasoned, *a lot should help more.* And I needed all the help I could get.

COVID-19 had just shut the world down. That morning, we had done church online—twenty-five people watched. Which was a bummer when eight hundred had shown up in person the month before. While watching, I opened my inbox and saw two new emails.

1. Someone who was mad we stopped doing in-person services.

* Combining that type of breath work with ice baths (or any sort of water activity) is a bad idea—don't do it.

2. Someone who was mad we were thinking about returning to in-person services.

It was a strange time to be alive—and I was searching for a way to cope.

I shot out of the ice bath after the second round of breath work and reached for my towel with a shivering hand. Next up, a two-minute breath hold. I steadied my mind but immediately thought about how much more relaxing the practice would be if I was outside in my backyard with my bare feet on my lawn. After all, *if a little helps, a lot should help more.*

Blood rushed to my head as I hobbled through my kitchen, my body screaming for oxygen. I somehow managed to grab my journal, open the slider, and step onto my back porch without breathing. I placed the chair in the grass as I felt the warm sun on my face.

Then I went to sit down, and that is the last thing I remember.

Heliocentric Versus Geocentric Spirituality

The year 1543 was a big one for Nicolaus Copernicus. For starters, it was the year he died. But it was also the year his most important book was published: *De Revolutionibus Orbium Coelestium* (*On the Revolutions of the Heavenly Spheres*). He got to see the finished product on his deathbed and was delighted to know his life's work would outlive him.[2] In it, he proposed a radical idea.

Some called it dangerous.
Others said preposterous.
Most didn't give it a second thought.

But this simple idea changed everything.

The Idea: The earth is not the center of the universe.

Until that point, just about everyone assumed we were the middle of everything. The moon, sun, stars, and planets all revolved around us. *A geocentric model* is the technical term in case you want to sound smart at your next dinner party.

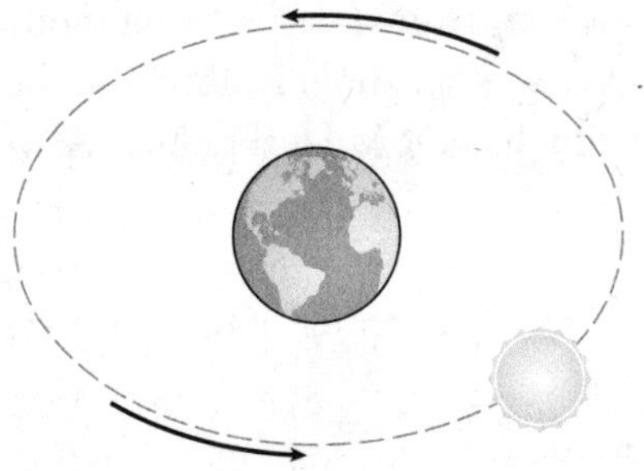

Copernicus offered up something different—a heliocentric model—in which the sun is the center of the universe and we earthlings (along with all the other planets) orbit it.[3]

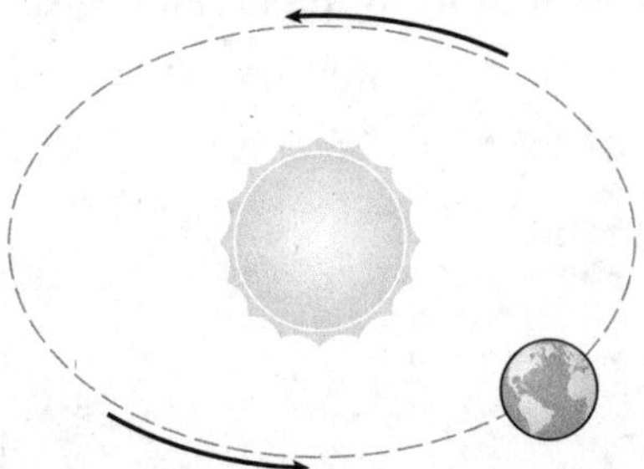

As you can imagine, the idea was met with more than a little resistance. Back then, people were pretty hesitant to embrace new ideas, especially ones that involved taking ourselves out of the center of the story.

And that brings us to today. This book is my best attempt to propose a similar idea.

Some will call it dangerous.
Others will say preposterous.
Most won't give it a second thought.

But this simple idea has the potential to change everything about your life.

My idea is not new—far from it. Jesus said it thousands of years ago. And many have written about it since. But these days, in the age of hyperindividualism, it will feel radical. Are you ready? Here goes. . . .

The Idea: The self is not the center of the universe.

I know. I know. Radical.

But while it may be easy to agree with that statement in theory, it's difficult to live like it's true.

The Bible starts with four really important words: "In the beginning God . . ."[4]

Not you.
Not me.

In the beginning *God*.

The Creator, the center of it all, then began creating. The most important of all his creations was us—humans, made in his image. Yet for a number of reasons we're about to dive into, we are really good at trying to put ourselves at the center of the story—sacrificing our mental health, good nights of sleep, and overall well-being in the process.

I call it *the unrelenting pressure of self-centeredness.*

Do you believe God is at the center of all of this?
Or do you put yourself in that place?

It may seem like a silly argument over semantics, but nothing could be further from the truth. It's two drastically different ways to live that head in opposite directions. At least, that's the working theory I came up with that day in my backyard.

I woke up facedown and lifted my head out of the grass, trying to find my bearings.

My left knee was bleeding.
My right elbow hurt.
Fortunately, all my teeth were intact.

I brushed away the bug making its way up my neck and glanced over at the patio chair lying on its side as if a giant gust of wind had just come through. But there wasn't any wind—just a guy who took self-help too far and passed out in his own backyard.

Once I managed to sit up, I shook my head and grimaced at the pain in my neck.

The irony was too good to ignore. If someone had walked by and seen me sprawled out, facedown in my backyard, they probably would have assumed I was some strung-out guy coming off a bender.

Nope.
I didn't overdose on drugs.
I overdosed on self-help.

It turns out, just because a little helps doesn't mean a lot helps more. And I realized, in addition to being very embarrassing, that was a helpful illustration of a very peculiar problem we have on our hands—so I grabbed my journal and started scribbling:

Every era of the church has its own unique set of challenges. I'm sure each generation thought theirs was the hardest, but ours feels extra strange.

The problem is me.

It's you.

It's the self.

If I was healthy, I would've gone for a walk, put God back at the center, and then (free from the pressure of holding this whole world together) let myself feel what I was trying so hard to avoid:

What if the pandemic shuts down the church?
Does that mean I'm not enough?
What about all those other pastors I compare myself with?
I'm scared.
I'm sad.
I'm tired.

And then, if I was healthy, I probably would've cried for a bit. Instead, I held my breath until I passed out.

In a chaotic season, I fell into the trap of putting myself back at the center of the story and inherited all the pressure that came with it. The longer I sat there thinking about this predicament, the clearer the picture of geocentric versus heliocentric spirituality became.

We are created to worship God.
But we are worshipping ourselves.

We are created for community.
But we are moving toward isolation.

We are created in God's image.
But we are obsessed with self-image.

It's becoming increasingly difficult to stop thinking about ourselves. And ironically, all the talk about self isn't helping us feel any better about ourselves—quite the opposite.

When self is at the center, your own little kingdom is constantly under attack:

Conflict threatens your self-image.
Critique threatens your self-esteem.
Mistakes threaten your self-righteousness.
You take everything personally because everything feels personal.

As a result, we end up with a world where everyone has thin skin but strong opinions. Self-centeredness is causing love to grow cold. It all feels eerily similar to Paul's prophetic words in his final letter to his protégé Timothy:

> People will be lovers of themselves, lovers of money, boastful, proud, abusive, disobedient to their parents, ungrateful, unholy, without love, unforgiving, slanderous, without self-control, brutal, not lovers of the good, treacherous, rash, conceited, lovers of pleasure rather than lovers of God.[5]

But it doesn't have to be that way.

Jesus demonstrated a radically different approach to life.

In a world of self-obsession, he spent his time serving.
In a world of self-righteous religious leaders, he hung out with the outcasts.
In a world of self-preservation, he laid down his life so we can go free.
In a world fixated on self-image, he showed us what it looks like to be made in God's image.

My thought is simple.

If we can shift from a geocentric model (self at the center) to a heliocentric model (God at the center)—or, to use more formal language, from anthropocentric (self at the center) to theocentric (God at the center)—it will change everything.

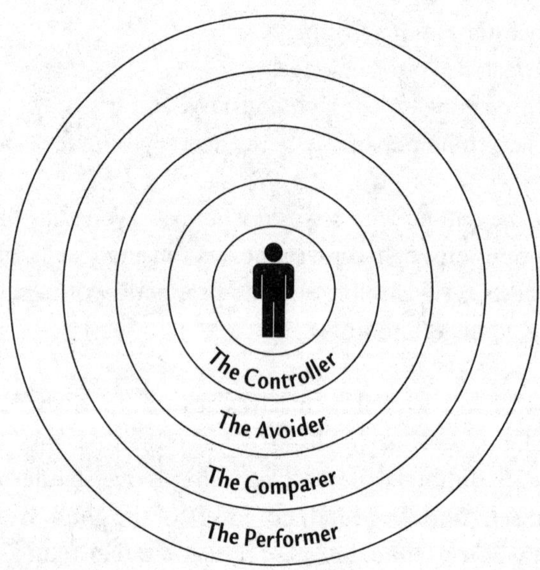

The Problem

Unfortunately, you aren't a blank slate. There are layers of residue from the old habits, beliefs, and pain in your past still moving you toward putting self back at the center of the story. Those layers cause you to perform, compare, avoid, and control.

Layer 1: The Performer

When self is at the center, it feels like there's a giant spotlight on you and it's your job to wow. In part 1, we'll talk about why that happens and what to do about it.

Layer 2: The Comparer

If **the Performer** is the puppet, **the Comparer** is pulling the strings. Self-centered spirituality throws us into the comparison trap. In part 2, we'll learn how to outsmart the part of us that can't help but compare our spirituality with our perceived competition.

Layer 3: The Avoider

Sink down another layer, and you realize the first two are simply games we play to avoid what's underneath. Fortunately, help is on the way. Part 3 is all about the Helper (the Holy Spirit), who heals in ways self-help never could.

Layer 4: The Controller

All the other layers are ultimately attempts to hold on to control. Control keeps us at the center of the story. In the final part, we'll discover the freedom of Christ-centered spirituality found on the other side of surrender.

I call getting lost in these layers the **me-maze.** Because despite your best attempt to see beyond yourself, those four roles you revert to are like walls that keep you stuck in a maze—thinking about you—weary and burdened from your attempt to carry the weight of the world on your shoulders.

The Goal of This Book

So, to begin, here's one biblical passage that raises many questions: "Do not lie to each other, since you have taken off your old self with its practices and have put on the new self, which is being renewed in knowledge in the image of its Creator."[6]

What's the old self?
What's the new self?
What are these practices?
And what does it mean that we're being renewed in knowledge in the image of our Creator?

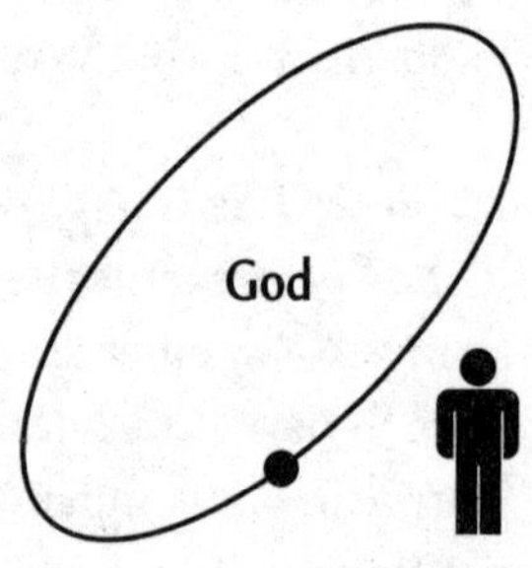

This book is about those questions—the antidote to self-centeredness is to take off the old self, put on the new, and be renewed in the image of God. Because an image bearer knows God is the center and their job is simply to enjoy being with God while reflecting God's glory to the world.

That's the goal of this book.

In his book, *Creator Spirit,* Steven Guthrie calls the Holy Spirt "the re-humanizing Spirit." He explains, "The Spirit is poured out on God's people, so that by the Spirit they may become truly and fully human, recreated in the Image of the perfect humanity of Jesus Christ."[7]

Re-humanizing is a great word, isn't it?

Jesus is the example of being fully human. As you put in the work found in these pages, the Holy Spirit will begin chipping away at the layers of your me-maze and you'll start feeling human again. Throughout the process, I'll give you three Christ-centered practices to help you take yourself out of the center of the story (for morning, midday, and evening).

This book is a guide to help you escape the maze of self-centeredness by embracing a God-centered life. Treat it like a handbook if you're feeling weary and burdened and ready to be "renewed in knowledge in the image of [your] Creator." When you do, you won't end up thinking less of yourself; you'll simply end up thinking of yourself less, and the unrelenting pressure of self-centeredness will begin melting off your shoulders.

That's what happened for me—what's still happening as I do this hard and countercultural work myself. I figured the most helpful thing I can do is take you through story after story of me getting it wrong. So before you start judging me for talking about myself in a book that's supposed to be about abandoning self-focus, don't worry. None of these stories are meant to show how great I am (quite the opposite, actually).

But along the way, I've been learning the power of our five-word prayer: *Lord, free me from me.*

It's time to escape the me-maze.

Copernicus offered a new way to think about astronomy. Scripture offers a new way to think about spirituality.

Rest for the soul is right on the other side of transferring all the pressure back over to a God who is more than capable of handling it.

If that sounds like a worthy journey to embark on, then let's begin.

Layer 1 | The Performer

From Self-Image to God's Image

Truth Statement: ***I am created in the image of God.***

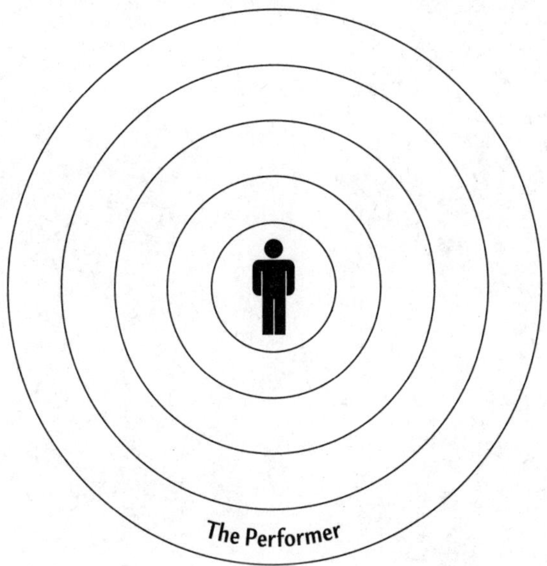

1.1: The Me-Maze (Part 1)

St. Patrick's Cathedral

We're all stuck in a me-maze, a self-created labyrinth leading ever inward that can only make us feel more lost. More confused. More crushed under pressure we weren't meant to carry.

You might hear the term *me-maze* and know exactly what I'm talking about. You may immediately think of a moment in your own past when you felt stuck in a similar place, whether because of circumstance, generational trauma, or emotional weight. Maybe you're in that place right now, wanting desperately to get out but feeling like every step forward is only taking you further into the maze.

For those of you who may not immediately resonate with the idea of the me-maze, allow me to offer a brief example, which is how we'll begin all four parts of this book.

Manhattan felt like a maze. The tens of thousands of buildings in it seemed to be banding together to obstruct my view and make me feel trapped.

Building after building.
Block after block.
Each busier than the last.

My friend Beej and I weren't meeting in Central Park until that afternoon, so I had the morning free. I was trying to get to the Morgan Library, but I was lost and the app on my phone was all but useless. That little blue line I was supposed to be following hadn't updated in five minutes.

No one was waiting until the light turned to cross. They would simply see an opening and walk. I tried to do the same, hoping to blend in. A loud horn filled my left ear, and I jumped back up on the curb, refusing eye contact with the driver.

I was a fish out of water. A tourist confused by an intuitive numbering system. And everyone knew it.

Are they staring at me?
What am I doing wrong?
Wait—what street did I just pass?

My heart rate was high.
My breath was short.
My chest was tight.

I was panicking in the wrong place at the wrong time, which made me worry even more—panic about panic.

Manhattan is a maze. But that isn't the maze I was stuck in. The maze I was stuck in is way more complex. It has more pathways (and these ones aren't numbered). This maze feels impossible to figure out, let alone escape.

The maze was me.

Have you ever experienced this?

Feeling like you're trapped in a maze of your own making? A maze with so many twists and turns that it makes Midtown Manhattan look tame? A place where you can get lost, not just for a day, but for an entire lifetime? Where your inner dialogue can be so mean that it makes an angry shop owner sound friendly? And where rest can be even scarcer than in the city that never sleeps?

The light turned red, and the Walk sign came on. I was the only one who hadn't already crossed—the teacher's pet who stayed back to follow the rules. I finally stepped out into the street, my chest tightening more with each step.

And that was when I saw it: St. Patrick's Cathedral—a majestic historic structure straight out of a movie. The building had a gravitational pull. It called to me.

I walked through the massive double doors and heard something I hadn't heard in several days: silence—or close to it, a disproportionate amount compared with the chaos a few feet away. As if the team who built the entrance in the nineteenth century knew we'd need a fortress to escape into on one of the busiest streets in the world.

The place was reverent—the architecture breathtakingly beautiful. Giant white columns reached toward the ceiling at least thirty meters overhead. Gorgeous stained-glass windows lined the sides. Pew after pew led up to a giant cross at the very end, with room for more than two thousand people (the curse of a pastor: We always know how many people can fit in a room).

Everyone was sitting down.
Mass was about to begin.

I panicked.

Wait—I'm not Catholic.
I'm a Protestant pastor.
Is this okay? (It was.)
What if someone sees me? (They won't.)
Will they care? (Care about what?)

I felt like I was wearing a straitjacket as I fought for every ounce of oxygen I could manage to gulp down. Mercifully, there was an empty pew near the back, far enough away that my lack of knowledge about standing and kneeling wouldn't distract anyone. (For years, I had stood on a stage and watched people sneak in the back mid-sermon, wishing they'd feel welcome and wondering why they looked so nervous. I was that guy now.)

I started thinking about the church my friends and I had planted five years earlier. As great as it was going, it was also a lot.

A lot of details.
A lot of people.
A lot of planning.
A lot of names to remember.
A lot of questions—most of which I didn't have answers to but believed I was expected to.

In short, a lot of pressure.

All things we signed up for. All things we prayed for. "Good problems to have," people loved to remind us. But good problems are still problems.

My loud thoughts were back to spinning. But this time, the panic wasn't just from the people on Fifth Avenue. The roots ran deeper. Spirituality had turned me into a performer.

The priest approached the podium. "The Lord be with you," he said.

"And also with you," I whispered.

"And with your spirit," the congregation said, drowning me out.

Dang it. 0 for 1.

The reading was from Genesis 2—the story about God creating the first human. "The LORD God formed a man from the dust of the ground."[1]

Something about being a pile of dust sounded funny to me.

Before all the fears.
Before all the worries.
Before all the comparison.
Before all the overthinking.
Before all the performing.
Before all the pressure.

We were just dust.

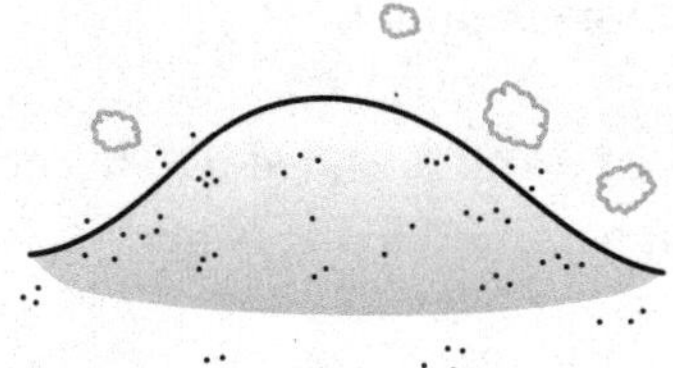

Do you ever take yourself too seriously? A pile of dust acting that powerful feels like a parody, doesn't it? Yet it also offers momentary reprieve from the pressure we like to put on ourselves.

As I sat in the cathedral, I imagined a pile of dust trying to carry the weight of the world's problems and then looking in the mirror, obsessing over its self-image.

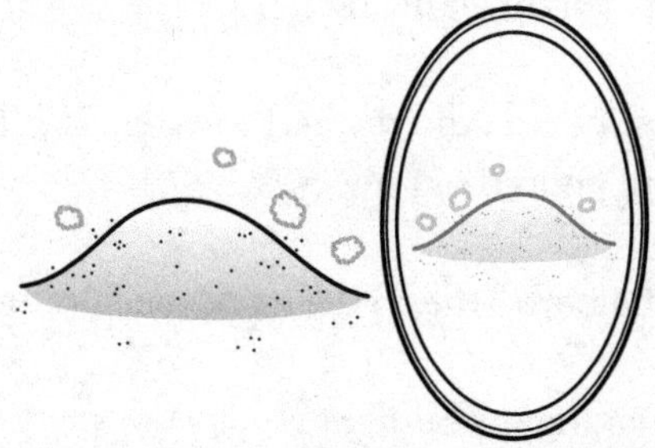

Or a pile of dust trying to perform its way into being accepted by an audience.

The image was comical.

My fists began to unclench.
My jaw relaxed.
My overactive mind slowed a bit.

The reader continued, "And breathed into his nostrils the breath of life, and the man became a living being."[2]

I pictured the Creator, the original artist, breathing into a pile of dust. God's exhale was our first inhale.

I inhaled deeply, one of those breaths that remind you how shallow your breathing has been of late. I wasn't sure if it was the scripture, the setting, or the lack of sleep, but the deep breath loosened the straitjacket around my chest. Air sank into my bound-up body, and oxygen flooded through my me-maze like a mighty river breaking down a dam. My shoulders dropped three inches, and tears fell down my face.

The reading continued. I did my best to listen. While months of pent-up pressure poured out my eyes.

"The Word of the Lord," the reader said, concluding.

"Amen," I said, taking my best guess.

"Thanks be to God," those around me corrected.

0 for 2.

Everyone stood.
I couldn't.
Not yet.

Thankfully, no one was judging me. Everyone understood. All of us humans with our own me-mazes to navigate.

I took out my journal and scribbled down some language in an attempt to process the moment:

I love church. Leading moments like this comes naturally to me. I can look around a room and intuitively know what people need. But apparently, I've lost the ability to be the one in the pew listening.

I've traded in studying Scripture for wanting to be the Bible-Answer Man. I've traded in talking with my Creator for wanting to be known as a person who prays a lot. I've traded in spirituality for an attempt to be perceived as the super-spiritual guy.

God's presence had become my performance.
Spirituality had become a means to an end.
And the end was my own self-image.
That's an awful lot of pressure.

But in that sacred moment—covered by a cathedral that has offered quiet refuge to millions, surrounded by a tradition that was here long before I showed up and will remain long after I'm gone, participating in one of the thousands of services since they opened their doors in 1879—I felt peace.

As if the cathedral was inviting me out of the center of the story.
And the unrelenting pressure of self-centeredness.

I noticed my surroundings.
The candles lit against the walls.
The smell of the incense.
The beauty of the city.

Gratitude filled my entire being.
And it brought me out of the me-maze.

The congregation shifted in their seats. I knelt, trying to fit in, while everyone stood.

Strike three.

Thank God I wasn't in charge.

It was the closing hymn.

Joyful, joyful, we adore thee.

I started singing, which surprised even me. I stared down at the picture of the me-maze I had sketched in my journal and thought about a movie I had watched in sixth grade about a sixteenth-century Polish astronomer named Nicolaus Copernicus. And his paradigm-shifting idea that we aren't the center of the universe. I realized I was doing the same thing at a personal level—the thing we're still doing at a global level: putting myself at the center of the story.

This tradition, for all its imperfections, pointed to a much deeper truth. The most important truth of all time. The truth that is at the root of breaking the me-addiction:

Beyond my own little temporary kingdom . . .
There is an eternal kingdom.

Called the kingdom of heaven.
That kingdom has a King.
And his name is Jesus.

Which means the weight of the world is not on my shoulders or your shoulders. The responsibility to get everything done is not all on me or all on you. Perfection is not something we have to master.

I drew a picture of Jesus at the center of the story. With us orbiting.

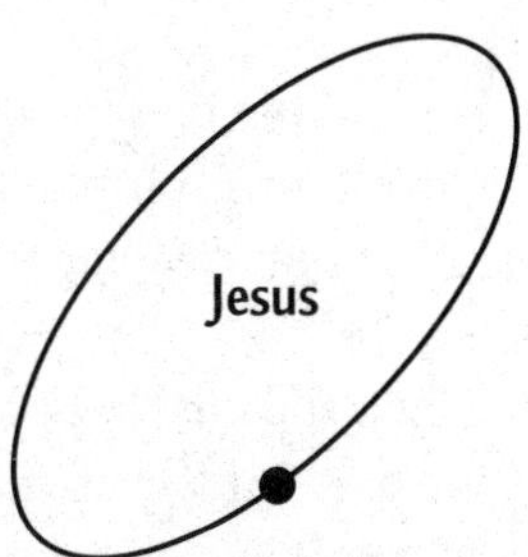

And jotted down a simple thesis I'd been working on ever since I passed out in my own backyard:

Jesus at the center leads to freedom.

Self at the center creates the me-maze.

And the never-ending pressure that comes with trying to figure it all out.

Lord, free me from me.

Then I headed back out into the maze of Manhattan.

The Performer

What really happened in that cathedral?
Where were the tears coming from?
Why were a random midday mass and a passage I'd heard a thousand times so moving?

I've become so curious about those questions that I've written this entire book about them. Because I'm so prone to get stuck in the me-maze and make spirituality about me.

And I have a feeling you can relate.

Because every time I tell someone about the me-maze, they nod and tell me their own version of how they do the same. It turns out, every human struggles with putting self at the center in their own way. Everyone is stuck in their own me-maze.

The weight of self-centered spirituality is real, and we need to talk about it.

For me, the number one tell that I'm stuck in the me-maze is when I turn spirituality into a performance to impress others rather than keeping it a practice to connect with God.

When spirituality becomes a performance . . .
We overthink every interaction.
We ruminate on every mistake.
We obsess over our self-image.

Our inner **Performer** puts an unrelenting amount of pressure on us.

One of the reasons this book is filled with so many of my failed attempts to take myself out of the center of the story is to show you just how complex the maze of self-centeredness can be. How normal it is to get stuck. As I mentioned in the introduction, I realized the best way to help you expedite your own escape would be for me to report on all the dead ends I've found along the way.

You've probably got your own stories to tell. Maybe for you it's also the pressure to appear spiritual. Or the pressure to be moral. Or the pressure to paint a smile on your face even though you're screaming internally.

I get it.
We all get it.

Whatever it is for you, the first step to journeying out of self-centeredness is to drop the act. Which raises the next question: *Why are we so tempted to perform in the first place?*

There are a few good answers to that question. After all, *me-maze* is just my language for a phenomenon that real professionals have talked about for years.

Psychologists have their own name for the me-maze.
And theologians have an explanation for where it came from.

In the next chapter, we'll talk about both, and it'll help us understand why spirituality can so quickly become a performance.

1.2: The Spotlight Effect

How Spirituality Becomes a Performance

The stars were out. It was a chilly Wednesday evening in Boulder, Colorado, and I was walking home from the library with David Crowder Band's new worship album blaring in my headphones—singing and thanking God for my life. I was in college, and after a wild series of events, faith was starting to really make sense to me.

When I got home, the door was open but no one was inside. Not because we got robbed but because we operated on what we called an open-door policy—where we never shut the door, so everyone knew they were welcome.

Not the smartest idea in the winter.
Not the safest idea ever.
But our prefrontal cortexes were still developing.

I dropped my bag, grabbed my Bible, and sat on our front porch under the stars, exhaling and watching my breath rise into the cold Boulder sky.

I was still fairly new to the Bible, so I was reading through the book of Romans with my friend Chris. That week, we were on Romans 8, and every verse was landing.

> Those who live according to the flesh have their minds set on what the flesh desires; but those who live in accordance with the Spirit have their minds set on what the Spirit desires.[1]

Walk by the Spirit.
Not by the flesh.

In my mind, I'd been doing a lot better saying no to the flesh, which to me, as a student at the number one party school in the country, just meant I wasn't partying as much as I used to. The gospel was taking root in my heart, and I was experiencing the transformation.

In the next breath, I realized how cold it'd gotten. As I got ready to go inside, a thought stopped me. *My roommates will probably get home soon.*

The thought started innocently. *They'll all be pulling into the driveway; I should stay here until they do.*

I pictured them getting home and seeing me having what we call a "quiet time." I thought about how impressed they'd be by me being out here in the cold spending time with the Lord. *They're gonna think I'm so spiritual.*

So I stayed put, closed my eyes, and turned on another worship song.

By the time it ended, the cold was almost unbearable. I was shivering and there were no roommates in sight. I got up, but then the thought came back. *What if one of them is hanging out with his girlfriend? Even better. She'll go tell her friends how Ryan prays under the stars.*

So I circled back with God about how good I was doing walking by the Spirit instead of walking by the flesh.

Which of course is all ridiculous. None of my roommates were driving home wondering, *Is Ryan reading his Bible today?*

No one would've cared if I was.
No one would've cared if I wasn't.
They were all busy living their own lives.

And in case you're wondering, the whole be-super-spiritual-to-impress-girls schtick never panned out.*

The more interesting questions are, *Why did I care so much? Why did a peaceful evening prayer suddenly become a performance? Why did I shift from spending time with God to wanting to be seen as the guy who spends time with God?*

And then there's the question beneath those questions: *Why do we go to such great lengths to protect our self-image?*

And the question beneath that one: *Why do we feel like everyone is only ever watching us?*

Psychologists have some thoughts.

A Psychological Name for the Me-Maze

Do you ever feel like your life is a movie and the whole world is sitting in the crowd, stuffing their faces with popcorn and Pepsi as they watch your performance? Whispering their critiques to their friends in the next seats.

That wasn't funny.
That was mean.
Why did they say that?

Psychologists call this "the spotlight effect"—our tendency to overestimate how much other people notice us. In one famous experiment, students wore embarrassing T-shirts and then walked into a room of peers. Afterward, they severely over-

* For more on this, check out my first book, *Single Today.*

estimated how many people noticed.[2] We all perceive that the spotlight is on us, even though everyone else thinks it's on them.

Psychologists talk about how we all have an egocentric bias. A bias toward seeing self as the center of every story. Which, if we're being honest, just makes a lot of sense. After all, you're perceiving the world through *your* eyes, not anyone else's.

But that bias causes us to overestimate our own importance in any given situation and thus put too much pressure on ourselves.

Except I'm not a psychologist. I'm just a lowly pastor. So instead of the spotlight effect, I call it the me-maze. Which is a phrase I made up, but when you're choosing to freeze out on your front porch to impress roommates who aren't home and don't care, *maze* sure seems like the right word, doesn't it?

Psychologists may've coined the phrase *spotlight effect* in 1999,[3] but this problem goes back to the very beginning. It's a psychological phrase that shines a bright light on a theological truth.

A Theological Explanation of the Me-Maze

The first two chapters of the Bible are glorious. In Genesis 1–2, God breathed his breath into us and called us good. At first, we were created beings who were content to put God at the center of the story and take our place as image bearers, but it didn't take long for everything to unravel.

Theologians call Genesis 3 "the Fall." It was the moment sin entered the picture and created separation between us and God.

But what really happened when Adam and Eve ate the fruit? The answer to that question is found in the lie the serpent spun. " 'You will not certainly die,' the serpent said to the woman."[4]

That lie was just a quick jab from the serpent before he threw his big left hook: "God knows that when you eat from it your eyes will be opened, and you will be like God, knowing good and evil."[5] That's the lie. A lie so rich that it does what every great lie does—raises dozens of other questions:

I can be like God?
Is God holding out on me?
Would I make a better God?

Let's give the serpent some credit; that's a pretty good lie. There's a reason John called him the father of lies—lies are his native language.[6]

Adam and Eve took the bait. Instead of trusting God's design as image bearers, they decided to define their own rules.

They were created in God's image.
Created to reflect God's glory.
But they decided they wanted to be the ones in charge.

And in that moment, it was like a giant spotlight shone down on them, exposing their flaws and following them everywhere. As though they had become the center of the story, the headliner everyone had come to see.

I like the way Christopher A. Hall says it: "Our thoughts about ourselves and the world we live in have been deeply warped in a number of ways, a curving and cracking of our personalities related to a fundamental lie first stated in the Garden: We must be at the center of things; we must be the kings and queens of the universe. Thus, we are skewed, *incurvatus in se* (curved in on ourselves)."[7]

Curved in on ourselves—or, as I like to call it, lost in the me-maze.

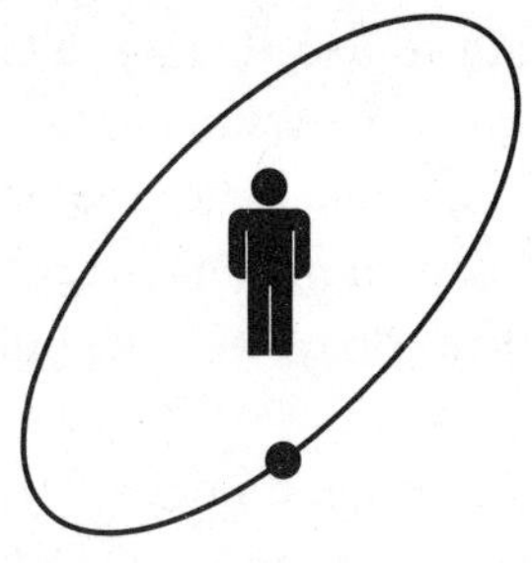

That's the origin of the me-maze (or spotlight effect) and the theological explanation for it.

But the most illuminating part of Genesis 3 is what happened next. Adam and Eve put themselves at the center of the story and were so overwhelmed with their shortcomings that they overcompensated by going into performer mode: "They sewed fig leaves together and made coverings for themselves."[8]

When the spotlight turned on, they ran to the costume box and pulled out the only thing they could find for their performance—fig leaves. Just as they were putting the finishing touches on their costumes, they heard God walking in the garden in the coolness of the day.

"Where are you?" God asked.

Adam tragically replied, "I heard you in the garden, and I was *afraid* because I was naked; so I hid."[9]

They ran.
They hid.
They sewed fig leaves together to cover up.

That's the moment this entire book is about. Because we replay that moment every single day. The spotlight comes on, we perceive that we are center stage, and we start singing for our supper.

The first performance wasn't all that spectacular.

The cast (Adam and Eve) spent more time blaming each other than supporting each other. The costume design (fig leaves) was lackluster. And the audience (God) wasn't convinced.

Of course, that was a long time ago, and to be fair, the performance was unexpected and rushed. Since then, we've had time to write much more compelling stories to hide behind and we've made tremendous upgrades in the costume department. Our fig leaves have become infinitely more robust.

Some use money.
Some use success.
Some use status.
Some use knowledge.
Some use influence.
Some use humor.
Some use morality.

Can you resonate with any of those fig leaves? If you're anything like me, your costume is a complex combination of several of them.

But at the end of the day, we're all doing the same thing—performing. You, me, Adam, Eve, and everyone else are attempting to put on such a spectacular performance that it merits the giant spotlight shining on us. And that is an awful lot of pressure.

Which takes us back to my front porch on that cold Boulder night. What I couldn't see then was that spirituality had become my new fig leaf.

The gospel was clicking.
The Holy Spirit was setting me free.
But then I wanted everyone to know it.

I don't just want to pray; I want to spend so much time praying that when I pray publicly, everyone knows how spiritual I am. I don't just want to worship; I want to be known as the guy who worships passionately. I don't just want to be morally good; I want to be seen as the guy who is strong enough to say no to the world.

It's exhausting.

Because sometimes the performance goes well and I get the validation I'm searching for. But most of the time, it doesn't.

Sometimes roommates show up and applaud.
Most of the time, they leave us out in the cold.

Lord, free me from me.

Fear over Love

Did you notice Adam's motivation for the performance? He told God, "I was *afraid* because I was naked; so I hid."[10] The Fall was the moment our motivation got a demotion—from love to fear.

Fear of being seen.
Fear of being known.
Fear of being exposed.

Mixed with a belief that a giant spotlight is shining only on us and everyone is watching. (Which of course isn't true. Other people are all busy dealing with their own spotlight, but in the moment, the spotlight feels like the truest thing in the world.)

So to recap, your greatest fear is to be fully known, but you perceive a bright spotlight shining on you—that's quite a combination. Which is why I'd wager your inner **Performer** has its own go-to routine.

Maybe for you it's wowing people with how much you know.
Or surprising people with how whimsical you are.
Or impressing people with how holy you are.

Fear causes us to perform.

We were created to reflect God's glory. But when we put self at the center of the story, we became obsessed with our own glory. We traded in God's image for self-image. And in the broken state we're in, that is about as vulnerable a feeling as you can ever experience, so we reach for fig leaves to try to cover up.

Spirituality is a go-to fig leaf.

You may not be as deranged as I am, so you may not freeze out in the cold for an extra twenty minutes on the off chance someone will come home and see you being spiritual, but I bet you have your own version of this. After all, since the Fall, every one of us is affected by the me-maze. At some level, we all feel like there is a spotlight on us.

Even C. S. Lewis once wrote,

> I catch myself posturing before the mirror, so to speak, all day long. I pretend I am carefully thinking out what to say to the next pupil (for his good, of course) and then suddenly realise I am really thinking how frightfully clever I'm going to be and how he will admire me.[11]

He wrote that to his childhood friend Arthur Greeves in a letter where he humorously estimated every third thought he had was about self-admiration.

Lewis had his own list of how he tried to perform.
I've got mine.
You've got yours.

This is where our prayer (*Lord, free me from me*) starts taking us on a journey.

If you're serious about God answering that prayer in your life, the first step is to get really honest about your list. Once you start naming fig leaves, you'll probably realize you have way more than you thought.

Take a moment and start a list (I literally have a note in my phone titled "Fig Leaves"). Begin naming the metaphorical fig leaves you tend to hide behind and then, whenever you notice another one, add it to your list.

My list is long and a bit frustrating. If you're feeling discouraged, here's an important addendum: *It's not your fault.*

Or at least, not entirely.

There are psychological and theological reasons we put self at the center, but it's more than that; there are also cultural reasons. This rise in self-centeredness didn't come out of nowhere.

As we go, I'm going to continue helping you understand the problem theologically (fig leaves and hiding is only the beginning), but I also want to help you understand the problem culturally.

Next up, a chapter about a massive shift that has happened over the last few centuries, because understanding the cause of the problem will help us see the solution. So it's time to talk about the Enlightenment, the Romantics, and a breakfast I had with my friend Keith.

1.3: The Problem with Being the One in Charge

A Cultural Reason for Self-Centeredness

The diner was exactly how you might picture it—simple menu, old-school booths, and a waitress named Judy who was hitting me with a "Freshen up your coffee?" every five minutes. My answer to that question is always yes, so it could have been the caffeine surging through my veins, but I was locked in on every word Keith was saying.

"The concept of self is a relatively new idea," he said between bites of bacon. "That is, if by 'self' you mean personal identity. You can trace it back to the Romantics."

I nodded, pretending to know who the Romantics were but making a note to google it later.

Breakfasts with Keith are dangerous—they usually turn into brunch. On this particular day, it turned into lunch. Got there at ten. Left at two. (Because I know some of you just panicked: Yes, I tipped extra. And no, people weren't waiting for our table.)

I had told him about my experience in St. Patrick's Cathedral, the me-maze, my idea to write a book about being addicted to self, and how I didn't know where the book was supposed to go next. That was all he needed to jump into a brilliant riff about the Romantics that I was doing my best to keep up with.

Thankfully, Keith is a gifted teacher. He spotted the insecure nod from a mile away and backed up.

"Think back to the Enlightenment in the seventeenth and eighteenth centuries," he explained. "We call it the age of reason. The time we learned how to think through our problems rationally. A lot of important shifts began during those years. It's when individuals started using logic and science to come to conclusions about the world."

"Right," I said, scribbling in the journal I keep close by anytime Keith gets going.

"Well, toward the end of the eighteenth century, there was an artistic revolt against the Enlightenment—we call them the Romantics. And this is way too simplified, but in a time of reason, science, and progress, the Romantics were the ones who felt confined. They began creating art that prioritized emotion and a desire to express themselves."

"Sure," I said, remembering bits of that from school. "But what does art have to do with our obsession with self?"

"It wasn't the art; it was the focus of the art," Keith said patiently. "Romanticism was about self-expression. So naturally, their focus shifted from the group to the individual. That may not sound like a big deal today, but that's because we're used to it. Back then it was radical. A shift that began to expand way beyond art—that many experts believe is a key contributing factor of the invention of the modern self."

"Freshen up your coffee?" Judy asked.

"Of course," I said and then turned back to Keith. "So, what started as an artistic revolt against logical thinking morphed into a desire to express the self, then snowballed into a mainstream phenomenon?" A watered-down interpretation of his already watered-down explanation.

"Essentially," Keith said, smiling. I knew he was resisting explaining all the nuances. "And with that came an emphasis on personal identity—finding meaning and identity in yourself—what we call today expressive individualism."

From there, Keith's riff turned into a brilliant lecture, taking me on a tour of this word *self,* linking Romanticism to modern psychology in a long, fascinating explanation of how we've elevated the self over the group, personal feelings over collective values, and authenticity over authority.

We talked about the pros of this shift. How learning to think for yourself and feel your emotions is a great thing. We talked about Genesis 1–2 and how a high view of self is not sacrilegious but scriptural—after all, we are created in the image of God (more on that soon).

Then we got to the cons. I told him about my idea to start the book with Copernicus, and he connected the dots for me.

"Right, so that's where this all becomes problematic," he said, now in full-on teacher mode. "The majority of the population used to think truth existed in an external source like God."

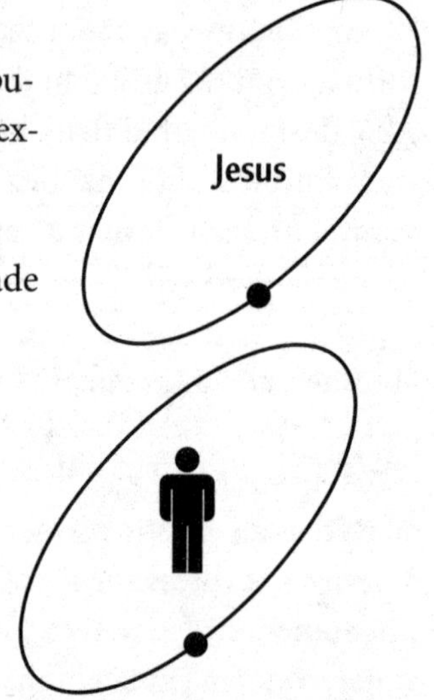

"Over the last few centuries, we've made an enormous shift. Today a vast percentage of the population searches for truth internally."

" 'Live your truth,' 'you do you,' and all the other anthems of our day," I added, trying to convince Judy I deserved to be in this conversation in case she was eavesdropping. “It’s the same mistake they made in the garden. We’re trying to define good and evil for ourselves.”

“Exactly. We want to be the one in charge,” Keith said, landing the plane. “But the problem with being the one in charge is you are the one in charge. Because if everything depends on you, then everything depends on you.”

Five cups of coffee later, I drove away with my head spinning.

I’m no psychologist or sociologist, but I am a pastor. And for more than a decade, I’ve had the same pastoral meeting hundreds of times. There seems to be a common denominator for just about every problem anyone goes through.

Me.
You.
The self.

We’ve moved from a heliocentric model—God at the center.
To a geocentric model—self at the center.

Now we are all caught in our own little me-maze, where we’ve traded in God’s image for an obsession with self-image. And where we feel the outrageous pressure that accompanies being at the center of the story.

Because the problem with being the one in charge is you are the one in charge.

Expressive Individualism

The deeper you dive into the subject of self, the more obvious the cultural shift away from a God-centered worldview toward a self-centered worldview becomes.

Carl Trueman sums up the Romantics this way:

> In short, the Romantics grant an authority to feelings, to that inner psychological space, that all human beings possess. And those feelings are first and foremost genuine, pristine, and true guides to who human beings are.[1]

We've given authority to feelings. They've become *true guides.* So . . .

Follow your heart.
Live your truth.
You do you.

And what started as an artistic rebellion of self-expression eventually spread far beyond art into popular culture.

In his massive book (both in size and importance), Canadian philosopher Charles Taylor talks about this shift:

> As well as moral/spiritual and instrumental individualisms, we now have a widespread "expressive" individualism. This is, of course, not totally new. Expressivism was the invention of the Romantic period in the late eighteenth century. . . . What is new is that this kind of self-orientation seems to have become a mass phenomenon.[2]

In other words, what was birthed out of Romanticism is now commonplace.

Expressive individualism is no longer reserved for the artist splitting a studio apartment with three friends in Manhattan, scraping to get by but feeling alive because she gets to express herself.
It's also for the investment banker who argues in boardrooms all day and then asks, *Who am I?* late at night in his high-rise apartment.

And the stay-at-home mom in the suburbs who spends her child's nap time pursuing a passion project.
And the loyal employee who has been crunching numbers for decades but recently told his boss he needs to leave his job to find himself.

Expressive individualism is now a priority not just for the poet but also for the plumber.

And please hear me (what I'm about to say is so important that I'm stalling to make sure you are with me): Pieces of this shift toward expressive individualism are a good thing.

Yes, God made you on purpose for a purpose.
Yes, you are fearfully and wonderfully made.
And no, I'm not proposing that we need some regressive demotion of the self where we knock off all the affirmations and start thinking we're trash.

God has more for you than that. So what's the problem with expressive individualism? Is the issue expressing yourself? Of course not. After all, the universe is an expression of the Creator. This whole existence is God expressing himself. And since you are created in God's image, you are created to express yourself.

Is the problem being an individual? Also, no. After all, you *are* an individual.

The problem is the starting point—when you begin your search for meaning with the self, you end up on the wrong trail. If the starting point for your identity is you, you'll end up obsessing over your self-image instead of reflecting God's image.

Expressive individualism platforms the old self. It preaches that you should be you, without first inviting you to die to yourself. It inspires you to be who you are, without first helping you see that you are a broken human like the rest of us.

Every construction worker worth their salt will tell you the foundation of a building project is essential. Without a firm foundation, you might as well tear the rest of the house down and start over.

Expressive individualism sets self as the foundation as you try to figure out who you really are, and self is about as shaky a foundation as you can have.

Welcome to the me-maze.

The good news is, when God is your foundation and you place him at the center of the story, you can take your place as an image bearer. You can spend your days reflecting God's glory as a freed-up image bearer, learning who you are.

Put simply . . .
When it's all on you, you anxiously obsess over self-image.
When it's all on God, you joyfully reflect God's image.

Think of the two options Jesus gave at the end of the Sermon on the Mount.[3]

Build your house on the sand.
Or . . .
Build your house on the rock.

In both scenarios, the wind and rain come. However, only the house built on the rock remains standing.

Feels timely, doesn't it? Almost as if Jesus knew the cultural shift toward expressive individualism was coming:

We packed up our house built on the rock—God at the center.
And moved down to the sand—self at the center.

Then the wind blew, the storm came, and we all got really mad at one another. When we convinced ourselves our truths were objectively true, other people's truths became a threat.

So we exposed one another.
And canceled one another.
And killed one another.

Difficult cultural questions created polarized shouting instead of illuminating conversation.

"Live your truth" sounds sophisticated and enlightened when there are no stakes involved. But played out in reality, with real people who have real trauma creating "truths" that completely contradict somebody else's "truth," the result is dividing at best and horrifying at worst. God's great dance floor turns into a vicious game of bumper cars. A bunch of humans—all caught in their own me-maze—bumping into one another while staring at a device that is encouraging the behavior.

We placed self where it doesn't belong. And now we struggle to take ourselves out of the center of the story.

So many of the challenges we face today are a direct result of being stuck in the me-maze.

We placed ourselves at the center.
We encouraged others to do the same.

But to quote my friend Keith, "The problem with being the one in charge is you are the one in charge. Because if everything depends on you, then everything depends on you."

At this point, you may be feeling hopeless. Because to recap part 1 . . .

There's a theological reason we put self at the center.
There's a psychological reason we put self at the center.
And there's a cultural reason we put self at the center.

Are we doomed to try to be at the center of the story for the rest of our days? Destined to perform under a giant spotlight, feeling a ridiculous amount of pressure? Stuck spiraling in the me-maze until the day we cross over into eternity?

No.

We can get out of the me-maze. We can make the shift from being self-centered to being God-centered.

How?

I'm glad you asked. The good news is, the answer is one word. A single word you'll spend the rest of your life trying to practice.

Worship.

1.4: Worship

The Scandalous Freedom of God-Centered Worship

"God, we welcome you in this place," I prayed passionately, hoping my volume would compensate for my lack of knowledge. "We just ask you to move."

After a winter of cold quiet times out on my front porch, trying to impress my roommates, I had spent the summer leading mission trips in Costa Rica. A job I had landed far before I was qualified.

That summer had been life changing.
Days full of serving and sweating.
Nights full of powerful (and very emotive) prayer and worship.

Now it was a Friday night in Boulder during the fall semester, and I was awkwardly trying to re-create one of those nights in my very secular college town . . . with about twelve people. It wasn't going well.

"Lord, you are welcome here," I practically shouted.

"But also," a girl shot back from the other couch, "we know you are always here; you are everywhere."

"Yeah," I rebutted, ego puffing up. "But, Lord, we're ready for the new thing you are ready to do, and so just to reiterate, we definitely do welcome you here."

"Yes, and," she fired back as if this were improv, "we don't want to talk about you like you aren't in the room."

I missed my missionary friends—the real Christians.

This argument went on for a few more minutes while the rest of the college kids wondered what they were doing there on a Friday night.

I was trying to usher in the presence of God.
She was trying to remind us God was already there.

I was convinced I was right.
She was convinced she was right.

Neither of us had the maturity to realize we may both have been seeing a piece of the puzzle. Instead, we continued triangulating our argument through God.

My friend Zach began the next song. I stood up, inner **Performer** fully activated, and started singing a bit too loud. (Also, as you continue painting this picture in your mind, note that I'm a really bad singer.)

One of my roommates got home. He walked through the front door. Looked around. And walked back out.

The other students on the couch watched him leave, wishing they could join.

As humorous as our little prayer debate was, it did bring up a good question:

Is God everywhere?
Or does he move about the world?

Who was right?
Me with my passionate plea?
Or her with her high view of God's sovereignty?

The answer, of course, is yes.

She was right because God is omnipresent. I was right because there are moments all throughout Scripture when God's manifest presence shows up.

But we were both wrong because we spent a night dedicated to worshipping God trying to outsmart each other.

The night was about God.
I made it about me.

Lord, free me from me.

When that song ended, it became abundantly clear that enough was enough. I thanked everyone for coming and retreated to my front porch (the same one I liked to freeze on in the winter months to prove to my roommates that I was spiritual) and stared up at the night sky.

I was tired.
I was frustrated.

And Jesus's words "Come to me, all you who are weary and burdened, and I will give you rest"[1] sounded like a foreign language to me. Because I thought I had. I had convinced friends to forsake the parties and instead worship in my living room. But apparently it hadn't worked.

Because instead of finding rest, I had stumbled into the unrelenting pressure of self-centeredness. I had tried to manufacture a moment. And when I didn't get the emotive response I wanted, **the Performer** took over. I say this with nothing but love for my younger self, who was doing his best, and grace for my current self, who still probably does similar things at times, but I put myself back at the center of the story.

And that is always the danger of worship.

What Is Worship?

Ask someone walking out of a church what worship is, and they'll probably say, "Oh yeah, that's the songs we sing before and after the message." And while that's certainly part of it, the word is way bigger.

Worship is life with God at the center. Singing is just one of the strategies we use to achieve that end. Yet even singing songs to God can become about self.

Worship of God . . .
Can become worship of self.

When the inner **Performer** takes over and convinces you to worry more about self-image than God's image.

Do you ever experience that? Either on the side of not wanting to look too spiritual:

Will it look funny if I raise my hands?
Am I singing too loud?

Or on the side of wanting to look super spiritual:

Do I look holy enough?
Will people think I'm good at this?

Both sides are **the Performer** still trying to control the narrative. And by the way, it's all completely normal—go easy on yourself.

My favorite definition of *worship* is "an act of ascribing ultimate value to something or someone."[2] In other words, whenever you take something that is good and make it the ultimate thing in your life, you are worshipping that thing.

We want to worship God.
But then sometimes we end up worshipping money.
Or safety.
Or a job.
Or a sports team.
Or reputation.
Or self-image.

Which is why some people retire, play two rounds of golf, and then spiral into an existential crisis. Or why grown men can become emotionally affected by a team they aren't even on.

The question isn't, *Do you worship?*
The question is, *Who or what do you worship?*

G. K. Beale surmises that Adam and Eve were in a constant state of worship while they were in the garden before the Fall in Genesis 3.[3] Not that they were singing "How great is our God" every second of every day. But rather that they existed in a constant state of understanding the premise of this book: that God is at the center and they were created in his image to reflect his glory.

So when Adam was naming the animals, he was doing it to reflect God's glory.[4] When he and Eve were working the land, they were doing it to reflect God's glory.[5] They were in a constant state of "do[ing] it all for the glory of God."[6]

I love that idea, because if you then turn to the very end of your Bible, you see that worship is a central theme of where all of this is heading. In Revelation 7:9–10, people from every nation, tribe, and language are crying out, "Salvation belongs to our God, who sits on the throne, and to the Lamb."

At the beginning of the story, it was a constant state of worship.
At the end of the story, it will be a constant state of worship.

But we live between those two moments, when it's really easy to put ourselves back at the center of the story. Which means we have to take intentional steps throughout the day to remember that God is on the throne. And again, there are lots of ways to do this. Singing is the most practical avenue, but you can learn to worship God in everything:

Enjoying a good bite of food can be worshipful.
Pausing to watch a sunset can be worshipful.
Building Legos with your kids can be worshipful.

Worship is the act of making God the ultimate thing in your life. Of getting out of the center of the story and ascribing ultimate value to the One who is at the center.

But there's another layer. The layer I was struggling with on that Friday night in Boulder. A layer I still struggle with at times.

Worship can help you escape the me-maze, but it's all too easy to let the inner **Performer** keep you stuck even within the act of worship.

If the devil can't get you to stop worshipping, he'll try to get you to make the worship about you. That was his strategy with Jesus during their epic showdown in the wilderness.

Jesus and Worship

Before he began his ministry, "Jesus was led by the Spirit into the wilderness."[7] He fasted forty days, and then he was tempted by the devil. For his final temptation, Satan took Jesus up to the top of a very high mountain and told him to look out over the kingdoms of the world. Then he made his offer: " 'All this I will give you,' he said, 'if you will bow down and worship me.' "[8]

Satan offered him the world.

Fame.
Fortune.
And all the things the flesh desires.

Using worship to become famous—that's the ultimate temptation of self-centeredness.

Jesus passed the test with flying colors, dropping a line we should not just read but memorize: "Away from me, Satan! For it is written: 'Worship the Lord your God, and serve him only.' "[9]

Instead of weaponizing his worship to enhance his performance, Jesus declared, "It is written: 'Worship the Lord your God, and serve him only.' "

But actually doing that isn't easy. **The Performer** doesn't go quietly into the night.

And that takes us back to that fatefully embarrassing moment in Boulder. My intentions were pure, but my **Performer** was still calling the shots. As a result, I was putting all this pressure on the night and making everyone uncomfortable.

True worship does the exact opposite.
It pulls you out of the center of the story.
And puts God back on the throne.

When we start praising, the walls of the me-maze start coming down.

As we continue to be transformed into the image of Christ, worship will become more and more natural to us. It'll stop feeling like a forced thing we do at church for a few minutes a week and start to feel like the thing our souls were created for. Eventually, it'll become more natural than anything else.

One day, when you take your final breath, you'll experience the fullness of that reality, but you don't have to wait. You can begin to step into that reality today. Because every time you worship, you are reminding yourself who you really are and what you are created for—being an image bearer. The ultimate antidote to an addiction to self-image is to take up your vocation as a person made in God's image—to worship the One who created you.

That last sentence is really important, so let's take a whole chapter to understand what we mean (and don't mean) by "image of God."

1.5: Image of God

You Are Neither Dust nor Divine

By this point, you should be starting to understand where the panic and tears were coming from that day in Manhattan. How I had once again turned spirituality into a performance. But more importantly, I'm hoping all these stories and analogies are helping you see that you're prone to do the same thing.

After all, this book is about you.

Which brings up a good question: *Who are you?*
Seriously. I'm not asking about your friend or your dog.
Who are you?

Answering that question might be tougher than you think. You may say your name, but that's not you. It's an identifier your parents chose to get your attention. You may start talking about your job, but that's not who you are; that's what you do. So then you might talk about your passion project or your purpose for being on the earth. And we're getting closer, but *why* you are here is still not the question.

The question is, *Who are you?*

Getting to the bottom of that question is hard. Most worldviews attempt an answer, but of all the ideas out there, the first few pages of the Bible offer the most compelling answer. They tell you who you are. But they also tell you who you aren't.

Let's start with who you aren't.
You aren't *dust*.
You aren't *divine*.

You Aren't Dust

Take a really deep breath and hold it for a few seconds.

Do you feel that? The oxygen flowing through your body? That's the reminder that you are alive.

No matter what kind of day you're having.
No matter what kind of stress you're under.
No matter what kind of heartbreak you've been through, conflict you've faced, or loss you've grieved.

You are here—right now.

Take another deep breath and, as you do, reread the verse that made me cry in the cathedral:

> The LORD God formed a man from the dust of the ground and breathed into his nostrils the breath of life, and the man became a living being.[1]

You matter, and it has nothing to do with your accomplishments. You matter because you are more than matter, and the breath of life flows through your lungs. Until you get that, you'll get caught trying to perform your way into significance. **The Performer** will constantly be trying to accomplish enough to graduate from being "dust."

Because anyone with a smartphone is being told on repeat that they aren't enough.
Entrepreneurs tell us we aren't rich enough.
Models tell us we aren't attractive enough.
Therapists tell us we aren't aware enough.
Influencers tell us we aren't famous enough.
Travel bloggers tell us we aren't spontaneous enough.

And before we know it, we start to believe that if we don't wake up at 3 A.M. to run five miles barefoot and then buy and flip a house before we finish our morning sauna session, we aren't enough.

The Bible has better news.
You are loved.[2]
You are chosen.[3]
You are more than a conqueror.[4]
You are adopted as a son or daughter.[5]

You are alive. You have breath in your lungs. That's a big deal. When I'm caught in the me-maze, it's usually because I'm *not* thinking about just how big a deal it is.

Steven Guthrie says it this way: "The work of the Spirit is to bring dust to life and fill it with glory, in other words, to make us truly human, the image bearers of God."[6]

So, take a deep inhale through your nose and hold it for a count of three.

One. Two. Three.

The point of this book is to teach you how to think about yourself less. Ironically, to do that, you have to stop thinking less of yourself. Strategies to stop self-obsession usually involve focusing on just how messed up we are: *You aren't God, so get over yourself.*

But statements like that don't really work.
Because they are only half the story.

You don't need a lower view of self; you need an accurate view, a biblical view. Which means you have to realize you were a miracle long before you were a maze.

Before you read any further, take a moment and let God's Word remind you who you are.

(Seriously. If you just rolled your eyes, you're a lot like me. When books tell me to slow down, I speed up. Fair enough. But you're going to get out of this book what you put in. I dare you to try this.)

Take a really big breath and then read Ephesians 2:10 as you exhale:

> We are God's handiwork, created in Christ Jesus to do good works, which God prepared in advance for us to do.

Now take another deep breath and read Psalm 139:13:

> You created my inmost being;
> you knit me together in my mother's womb.

In case you still haven't gotten it, do the same with Psalm 139:14:

> I praise you because I am fearfully and wonderfully made.

You aren't dust. You are worth more than you could ever imagine.

I needed that reminder that day in New York. At the most basic level, the panic I was feeling was caused by all the pressure I had put on myself to perform. As if my worth was somehow validated only if I did a good enough job with my spirituality. I was applying for the world's validation, and spirituality was my résumé.

Trying to build a fruitful enough church to matter.
Trying to build a successful enough writing career to matter.
Trying to prove to myself and the world that I have what it takes.

Maybe you know the feeling.
Maybe you do the same thing in your own way.

If so, you, like me, need to be reminded once again that, beneath all the things you do, you have inherent, eternal significance. Let that be a deep inhale for a suffocating soul.

If we think we're just dust, we'll stay stuck in **Performer** mode. You aren't dust. You matter—*inhale.*

But that's only half of it.
The tears were coming from another place.
A less obvious place.

If the first mistake is thinking too lowly of ourselves, the second is thinking too highly.

You aren't dust . . . but you also aren't divine.

You Aren't Divine

Here's a strange truth about spirituality: It actually works. And I don't just mean it helps you on your inward journey of finding freedom and purpose; I mean it changes external things.

Your prayers change things.
Your presence changes things.
Your worship changes things.

After all, you aren't dust.

And that's really good news, but it also brings about a whole new temptation. The same temptation Adam and Eve fell for in the garden. The same temptation so many worldviews and religions have been formed around. The same temptation at the core of so many cults. The same temptation that trips up followers of Jesus all the time.

You can be like God.

The lie that promises so much life.
But delivers only death.

Because it's a one-way, nonstop ticket to the unrelenting pressure of self-centeredness. That thought invites you to sit down in God's seat, expecting it to fulfill you, and before you know it, you set an impossible standard for the self.

It usually goes something like this . . .

Your spiritual journey has a positive impact on someone else, which in turn makes you feel good. Then it happens again, and again, and again, and before long, you notice the power. Then, oh so subtly, some piece of you starts to believe that *you're* divine.

And of course, you learn the right words to say.
And you figure out the right way to say them.
And eventually spirituality becomes a performance.

Most of us don't say that out loud; we aren't even consciously believing it. We just start living as though it's true.

And then you spiral whenever something goes wrong. Or someone critiques you. Or your intelligence is challenged.

Can I give you some really good news?
You are giving yourself way too much credit.
And it's putting way too much pressure on you.

After all, you aren't divine.

On one hand, God breathing his life into us tells us we aren't dust; we are more valuable than that. And on the other hand, God breathing his life into us also tells us we aren't divine. We didn't create us; God did.

I love Owen Strachan's words in his book on humanity: "His [Adam's] existence was God-derived, God-dependent, Godward in every sense."[7]

We are *made* in the *image* of God—not equal to God. Without God, we wouldn't be here. Which means you aren't the one who has to keep this whole life thing going. It's not all on your shoulders. As long as you believe it is, you will obsess over your performance, ascribing way too much weight to other people's opinions of how you are doing along the way.

I always know I'm stuck in the me-maze when I start obsessing over other people's opinions of me:

Did he think that meeting was helpful?
Did she take that joke the wrong way?
Did they like the answer I gave them?
Did I get any more followers?

As if I'm crowdsourcing my self-esteem. Asking others to remind me I'm more than dust. I get so caught up worrying that I'm ultimately just dust that I swing the pendulum to the other side and start living like I'm divine.

Take a breath and exhale.
And then another one.

Every inhale is a reminder that you are here.
You are alive.
And that is crazy.

But then every exhale is a reminder that you aren't divine. You didn't make the sun come up this morning. And one day, after you've breathed your last, it'll still rise. Your job isn't to make the sun rise; your job is to take a moment and appreciate it when it does.

You aren't in charge. And that's good news, because the world is a mess.
Is it beautiful? Absolutely.
But is it also broken? Big time.

Each inhale is an invitation to enjoy the beauty.
Each exhale is a reminder that you don't have to fix all the brokenness.

The weight of this whole world isn't on your shoulders.

Exhale.

And so, our original question: *Who are you?*
You aren't dust.
But you also aren't divine.
You are something different—you are a human, created in the image of God.

Image of God

When you read the first page of the Bible, you'll notice a pattern. God spoke; creation responded; he called it good. Over and over again. For five days.

Which was all setting up the pinnacle of God's creation on day six when he said, "Let us make human beings in our image."[8]

From the beginning, God's plan has been to share his good creation with his image bearers.

The power of that word *image* (*tselem* in Hebrew) gets lost on us today. But in the ancient Near East, the word *image* was deeply connected with ruling.

G. K. Beale writes, "Ancient kings would set up images of themselves in distant lands over which they ruled in order to represent their sovereign presence. . . . Likewise, Adam was created as the image of the divine king to indicate that earth was ruled over by Yahweh."[9]

We aren't dust.
We aren't divine.
We are image bearers.

You are created in the image of God.

And here's the really important takeaway: *That truth isn't predicated on your performance.* You don't have to audition for your role as image bearer—it's who you are. The louder that truth becomes, the quieter your inner performer will be.

Make sense? Good. Then let's dive a layer deeper.

While it's true you aren't divine, so you don't have to audition for your seat at the table, you also aren't dust, which means what you do as an image bearer matters.

We are the representatives of God here on earth, the indication that the earth is the Lord's. Which is why God told the man and woman to "be fruitful and increase in number; fill the earth and subdue it. Rule over the fish in the sea and the birds in the sky and over every living creature that moves on the ground."[10]

The words you say and the things you do matter. And let's just be honest, we don't always image God well. We're all broken humans.[11] We've all had those moments that left us thinking: *That wasn't it.*

That joke didn't *image* God well.
That reaction didn't *image* God well.
That decision didn't *image* God well.

As we already discussed, those mistakes don't disqualify us from being made in God's image, but they're still a problem.

Fortunately, Jesus has us covered. First, he is our "atoning sacrifice"[12] covering our sins (much more on that in Part 2). But Jesus is also "the *image* of the invisible God"[13] meaning we have a bull's-eye to aim for. Jesus showed us what it looks like to be fully human. The best way to image God is to practice living like him.

Love like Jesus.
Serve like Jesus.
Forgive like Jesus.

Notice what all those practices have in common: They have very little to do with Jesus and a whole lot to do with how he treated other people. In other words, the more we practice living like Jesus, the less we'll think about ourselves. As we're being transformed into the image of Christ, the walls of our me-maze will begin to crumble.

I love Robert Mulholland's summary: "Spiritual formation is a process of being formed in the image of Christ for the sake of others."[14]

Why are we doing all this work to be formed in the image of Christ? It's for the sake of others. So we can love who the world tells us to hate, forgive who the world tells us to resent, and serve who the world tells us to ignore.

We are created to rule.
But we rule by serving.

Tim Mackie sums up our role by saying we're called to "rule the world as God's partners, but Jesus style: in the power of service, humility, and self-giving love."[15]

Lord, free me from me.

How do we escape the me-maze?

The answer is right in front of us. It's something we do twenty-two thousand times every day.

You exhale and embrace the beautiful truth that even with all your imperfections, you are made in the image of God.
You inhale and continue to be transformed into the image of Christ.
Then you repeat.

But there's a solid chance that last line just set off a warning sign in your spirit. *Oh no, here we go. I knew this book was going to turn woo-woo.*

Hold on . . . Breath prayer isn't a departure from Christian orthodoxy. When practiced correctly, it's a return to its roots. But only if you do it right. When you don't, you end up passed out in your backyard.

Let's learn the proper way to reclaim breath prayer.

1.6: Breath Prayer

A Brief Christian History of Breath and Prayer

Free me from me is such an important prayer to pray today for a lot of reasons, one of them being the growing popularity of new age and its accompanying practices. A broad way to think about new age is as a spirituality that gives authority to the individual.

So where Christians give authority to Scripture—new age gives it to the individual.
New age isn't about discovering *the* Truth; it's about discovering *your* truth—the natural outworking of spirituality that is inherently self-centered.

Prayer becomes manifesting.
Stargazing becomes astrology.
Worship becomes a way to raise your vibration.
Serving becomes an attempt to increase your karma.
Spirituality becomes about the self.

Which is great marketing in a world of self-obsession. The problem is, as long as self is at the center of the story, you're stuck with the unrelenting pressure of trying to be divine.

The glaring issue, of course, is that people are broken. When you try to build something off an imperfect person's subjective truth, things inevitably fall apart.

Religious structure is set up to help minimize the brokenness of the people involved. Obviously, that structure isn't perfect. We have plenty of stories of the structure falling apart. However, the wheels come off way quicker when there's no structure at all.

Think about the number of documentaries focused on cults that started with rebelling against power and structure. Eventually, whoever happens to have the most charisma in the cult somehow finds their way "unofficially" onto a pedestal, and then one day everyone realizes that person just wanted money, sex, power, or some combination of all three.

I have meetings all the time with people who got caught up in new age, and they usually say the same thing—it promised freedom but led to bondage. But then they discover (or rediscover) the wild, subversive truth of the gospel and the invitation to take self out of the center, and it sets them free.

So of course, it makes sense that they become wary of returning to anything that feels "new age-y."

Which brings me to a conversation I had with my friend Jared.[1]

Is Breath Prayer Wrong?

"What's been the most helpful spiritual practice for you recently?" Jared asked.

"Probably breath prayer," I said and immediately recognized the concern on his face.

He was sitting in my office after several years of being deeply entrenched in new age. So, his eyebrow raise was justified. Because lots of new age spirituality implements breath work.

We backed up and talked through Jared's past. But when he asked me again what spiritual practice I'd recommend, I gave him the same answer—breath prayer.

Because ever since the Creator breathed his breath into a pile of dust, breath prayer has been a deeply spiritual thing. Today you will take somewhere around twenty-two thousand breaths. Each one, according to Isaiah, is a gift from God.[2]

Noticing that Jared wasn't convinced, I told him about the Egyptian desert monks around the fourth century who developed the Jesus Prayer, a prayer based on two stories in Luke 18 and Mark 10.[3]

The first is the parable about the self-righteous Pharisee and the humble tax collector who both went to the temple. While the Pharisee showed off to God, the tax collector cried out, "God, have mercy on me, a sinner."[4] The second is about the blind man in Jericho who heard Jesus was nearby and shouted, "Jesus, Son of David, have mercy on me!"[5]

The Jesus Prayer is a combination of the two in which you simply repeat, "Lord Jesus Christ, Son of God, have mercy on me, a sinner."[6] These bold words force you to admit that you aren't in charge and offer you an invitation to repent.

Over the centuries, Christians began connecting the Jesus Prayer to the rhythm of breath. They'd practice repeating that simple prayer over and over again (or to use Paul's language, they'd pray it without ceasing).[7]

Inhale: Lord Jesus Christ, Son of God.
Exhale: Have mercy on me, a sinner.

Notice, the inhale is all about God's goodness.
And the exhale is all about taking the pressure off you.

Christians have been utilizing breath as a guide for prayer ever since. It's a practical way to "let the message of Christ dwell among you richly."[8]

As an aside, some Christians critique this practice today, fairly pointing out that Jesus warned, "When you pray, do not use vain repetitions as the heathen do."[9] Which I think is a good reminder, but Jesus said "*vain* repetitions." In my experience, there is a big difference between *purposeful* repetition to connect with God and *vain* repetition to check a box. Breath prayer, when practiced with intention, is done on purpose, not in vain. (Also, Jesus was critiquing public prayers people were doing for show. I've found the best way to practice breath prayer is in private. As Jesus said in the same passage, "Go into your room, close the door and pray."[10])

Okay, back to my meeting with Jared.

"That makes sense," he said. "It's just that breath work has taken me to some interesting places."

He then told me about a holotropic breath work seminar he went to where they essentially practiced breathing really fast for an extended period of time until he felt like he had an out-of-body experience. The rest of that story is his to share, but it probably won't shock you to discover the seminar was all about self. So, for Jared, connecting breath and spirituality felt like it was going to move him deeper into the me-maze instead of out of it. Which is sad because breath is deeply connected to spirituality.

I decided to offer an analogy.

"Spiritual practices are kind of like vehicles," I told him. "Vehicles take us places, but they don't dictate where we go. We do. You can use a car to get to work, but you can also use a car to go buy drugs."

He nodded, but I like to over-make my points.

"You can use a car to serve at a shelter or to go have an affair. The car doesn't determine where you go; the driver does. Breath is a vehicle. And while I don't sign off on all the places people use it to travel to, that doesn't mean the vehicle is necessarily wrong. The vehicle can take you to a spirituality centered on self or centered on Christ."

Jared agreed but had a follow-up question: "How do I make sure it takes me to the right place?"

"The same way Christians have been doing it for hundreds of years: Scripture. Just like the Jesus Prayer, which invites you to read those two stories in Luke 18 and Mark 10 and come out with two lines saturated in Scripture."

Inhale: Lord Jesus Christ, Son of God.
Exhale: Have mercy on me, a sinner.

"By the way," I added, "I love those lines because they are all about repentance. Repentance is getting off the throne and putting Jesus on it. Repentance is getting out of the center of the story and letting God lead. Repentance is the move from a self-centered life to a Christ-centered life."

At that, Jared started getting excited and wanted to try the Jesus Prayer together.

The first one was awkward.
The next one felt forced.
By round three, my mind quieted down.
We spent rounds four and five being grateful for God's grace and the power of repentance.

The Jesus Prayer is a great place to start, but you can practice breath prayer with lots of different verses—Romans 8:1; Luke 1:46–47; and (my go-to) Psalm 23:1: "The LORD is my shepherd, I lack nothing." (More on this at the end of part 1.)

From the beginning, God was the One breathing his life into us. Every breath you take is a reminder of your dependence on God; it's the antithesis of self-reliance.

Each inhale is an invitation to be grateful.
Each exhale an invitation to let go.

Each inhale a reminder that God's got this.
Each exhale a reminder that you don't have to perform.

Each inhale a reminder that you aren't dust.
Each exhale a reminder that you aren't divine.

And that is really good news.

Drop the Act

As I learned while sitting on the pew in St. Patrick's Cathedral, the whole performance act can be really tiring. And unless you're much holier than me, you probably know exactly what I'm talking about. Think about all the ways we try to convince the world we're more spiritual than we actually are. All the ways we try to earn people's applause with our wisdom. All the ways we try to help enough people to prove to ourselves that we have what it takes.

Exhausting, right?

Thankfully, God is the one in control. And ancient practices, while often imperfect, can help us remember this.

So when you practice breath prayer, letting the deep breaths calm your bound-up body, remember that God's Word is also alive and active, like a double-edged sword in the hands of the eternal surgeon.[11] When we listen, we can hear Scripture speaking to the depths of our souls, reminding us that we're not the center of the whole story, every room we walk into isn't an audition, and we're not at the mercy of other people's opinions.

And that is really good news.
It means we can drop the act.

Equipped with that good news, you're ready to let the outer layer of your me-maze crumble. As you read this last story about the moment I finally learned how to let **the Performer** die, notice how God begins chipping away at the outer layer of your me-maze.

Chip.
Chip.
Chip.

1.7: Let It Die

Finding Freedom from the Inner Performer

Cardboard boxes were stacked all the way to the ceiling of the claustrophobic office—the mess mirroring my mind. I didn't know whose office it was, but apparently, they didn't mind clutter.

Unfortunately, the boxes were the least of my worries. The walls seemed to be closing in around me. I felt like Luke Skywalker in that creepy trash compactor scene.

Inhale . . . 2 . . . 3 . . . 4.
Exhale . . . 2 . . . 3 . . . 4.

The church we had planted was five months old. It had been an amazing ride, but that day, I was panicking. I was about to preach—the spotlight quite literally about to be on me—and I was fairly certain my performance was going to flop.

The critics are going to have a field day ripping into this one. The reviews will be devastating.

The Performer in me was spiraling.

I could see the line of cars waiting to get into the parking lot. Loud music welcomed people downstairs. It was busier than usual.

Fifty people quickly became 100.
Then 150.
Then 200.

Every church planter's dream. That day, it was my nightmare. Not the church growth or life change. But what came with it. All the eyes on me. The opinions. My desire to be liked. And my fear of being critiqued.

This sermon's garbage.
People are going to hate it.
They're going to leave and look for a "real church."

My plan was to sneak out the back and quit.

"Where's Ryan?" The anxious voice flew down the hall, followed quickly by footsteps. "Has anyone seen Ryan?"

I knew it was the production team. I knew they had questions about my slides. *I can't even get my slides right.*

Inhale . . . 2 . . . 3 . . . 4.
Exhale . . . 2 . . . 3 . . . 4.

Each deep breath momentarily delayed the inevitable, but I couldn't quiet my anxious mind.

What will people think about my sermon?
What are they going to think about me?
Why did I wear this shirt?

Remember, our greatest desire is to be truly loved, but our greatest fear is to be fully known. And when we think a bright spotlight is shining on us, our inner **Performer** feels its number being called and begins its routine.

My inner **Performer** was betting the house on my sermon:

Will I get any laughs?
How about tears?
Will the church work?

These types of worries are exhausting, and I bet you can relate. Because sometimes people applaud. But oftentimes they don't. Which leaves **the Performer** feeling vulnerable and inadequate, immediately searching for another hit.

Inhale . . . 2 . . . 3 . . . 4.
Exhale . . . 2 . . . 3 . . . 4.

The voices trailed down the hall. I felt like a kid playing a silly game of hide-and-seek, but I couldn't help it. I didn't want them to see me like this. Not when I was supposed to be leading this thing. I wondered if I should go do something else with my life. Something that didn't involve public speaking.

On the next exhale, I closed my eyes, and a memory appeared out of nowhere. A memory from another time I was teaching the Bible in front of a bunch of people. Several years earlier in the Dominican Republic.

Seeds, Fruit, and Death

The raised hand when there isn't supposed to be a raised hand is one of the scariest things a young public speaker can ever see. Especially when it comes from the back of a dark room.

I tried to block it out and keep going.

My friend Ethan and I were in the Dominican Republic. We were taking a room full of future ministry leaders through the entire Bible in five days—no small task.

On the final day, I was plowing through Paul's letter to the church in Galatia—explaining what Paul called the "fruit of the Spirit": the love, joy, and peace that come with walking in step with the Spirit instead of being "led by the flesh."

Meanwhile the hand waved at me from the back.
Somebody had a critique.
The Performer in me puffed up.

I increased my volume, picked up my cadence, and began telling the room about the orange tree in my backyard.

"An orange tree doesn't have to try super hard to produce oranges," I said emphatically, hoping my volume would drown out the hand now waving frantically. "It's just what it does. So it is with the one who walks in step with the Spirit. Continue on the right path for long enough," I practically shouted, "and before you know it, you won't have to try to have love, joy, and peace. It'll just come naturally."

Not bad.
Or so I thought.
But the hand raiser disagreed.

"You've skipped a step." The voice was serious but not stern. It cut through the room, confident but not arrogant. "Water is important," the speaker continued as she made her way to the front. "Sunlight is important. But none of that means anything until there is death."

I glanced over at Ethan. He was sitting with our friend Rodney—the one in charge—and they were both laughing. He shrugged and gave me one of those "well, this is just gonna have to happen" looks.

Cool. Thanks, guys.

"I'm the captain now," the hand raiser said, looking me dead in the eye. (I'm just kidding—she didn't say that.)

"A seed that is planted in the ground is packed full of potential," she told us, commanding the room better than I had all week. She was small in stature but a spiritual giant. "All the potential lies dormant until the seed dies. New life only comes on the other side of death."

"Too many people want to bear fruit without first denying self," she continued. "A seed that does not die remains a seed. It's unpopular to say this today, but you have to die to self. There are some people in this room right now still holding on to things—dreams, desires, habits, self-image. Let it go; let it die. There's so much freedom on the other side."

I sat down, pulled out my notebook, and started scribbling. All week I'd had the opportunity to equip future ministry leaders with wisdom about God and the Bible, but instead, I'd made it all about my performance.

Lord, free me from me.

Self at the center is like a seed that hasn't died.
That hasn't been broken open.
When the seed hasn't died, we keep trying to perform.

Think about **the Performer** in each of us, which always wants to impress, shock, and beat everyone else. Whether by hosting the best parties with the most life-changing food and brilliant discussion, buying something we don't need to impress our friends, or crushing a lecture or presentation at work so that all the attendees or our co-workers will walk away thinking about how great we are.

How smart we are.
How funny we are.
How spiritual we are.

Let it go.
Let it die.
There's so much freedom on the other side.

Every conversation you have is another opportunity to let **the Performer** die.

Is the person right in front of you an audience member to perform for or a human being to love? Is your goal applause or connection? Are you formulating your response while they talk, gearing up to drop a wisdom bomb on them that will make them wonder how they were ever lucky enough to have a friend as wise as you? Or are you actually listening to them?

Your inner **Performer** may think the first option is what the world needs from you. But the older I get, the more convinced I am people just want the second option.

I like how David Augsburger sums it up: "Being heard is so close to being loved that for the average person they are almost indistinguishable."[1]

Less performing.
More listening.

Freedom on the Other Side

I opened my eyes. I was back behind the cardboard boxes, except everything was calm. It felt like someone had turned down the volume in my head. Placing the doubts, worries, and concerns back on their proper shelves.

The sermon I was about to preach was on Philippians 2. All about how Jesus stepped out of heaven for us, became a servant to all, and then laid his life down so we can go free. Wonderfully good news, really.

I had worked hard prepping the sermon, which was good and important, but at the end of the day, the point was all very simple. Despite what my inner **Performer** may have thought, my job was not (and still is not) to wow people or change their lives, but to tell them about the God who can.

I can do that.

That experience behind the cardboard boxes allowed my inner **Performer** to die.

And maybe it's time for yours to do the same. Maybe, in this moment, something similar is happening for you. An invitation to trade in an obsession with self-image for the reality of being made in God's image. Maybe it's time to let go of the ways you try to impress. Your desires for the world to think you are enough. The elaborate fig leaves you've created.

Let it go.
Let it die.
There's so much freedom on the other side.

Performing is the first way we try to handle all the pressure. It works for a while, but eventually it leaves us crying behind a stack of cardboard boxes.

That moment offered me two options:

Quit.
Or let **the Performer** in me die.

I chose the latter.

Using the cardboard boxes as support, I crawled back up on my feet, then took one more really deep breath and walked downstairs to tell a bunch of people about the best news in the world.

I dare you to do the same.

Now, that's only part 1. **The Performer** is just the beginning—the outer (and most public) layer of the me-maze. The performance is like the puppet trying to put on a show, but there's another layer beneath it pulling the strings: **the Comparer.**

Comparison drives performance. It's at the root of so much self-centeredness. So, we've got some more digging to do. In part 2, we're going to talk about comparison, atonement, serving, manifesting, and a whole lot more.

But first, a Christ-centered spirituality practice.

Christ-Centered Spirituality Practice

Morning: Breath Prayer

That deadline is coming quick.
Why did I make that joke?
My birthday is in a few weeks—are my best days behind me?

If you're anything like me, these types of thoughts are a typical wake-up call. As if they are all hanging out together at the starting gate of my mind, just waiting for the alarm to go off so they can rush in.

For you, maybe it's worry. You wake up and immediately start overthinking that meeting you've got at 2 P.M. Or panicking about that email you're certain is waiting in your inbox. Or stressing about that complicated relationship you're trying to figure out.

Or maybe it's shame from the past. You wake up and immediately kick yourself for a mistake you made a day ago. Or a week ago. Or a decade ago.

And before you know it, self is in the driver's seat and any attempt you make to pray is really just about you: "God, I've got a lot going on today. Please help. Thanks, bye."

The first few minutes of the day are an essential part of the Christ-centered spirituality journey. So how do we put God back on the throne right from the beginning of our day?

Years ago, I listened to an interview with an author I deeply respect named Dallas Willard. The interviewer asked him about his morning routine, and Willard said he began each day by working through each line of Psalm 23.[1]

Sitting with it.
Picturing it.
Letting it sink in.

The Twenty-Third Psalm is that famous one David wrote that begins with "The LORD is my shepherd, I lack nothing."

(By the way, that one line could fix everything all by itself. If we truly grasped it, this book wouldn't be necessary, because none of us would be caught in the me-maze.)

Every morning you have two options:

Option 1: Trust the Lord to be your shepherd.
Option 2: Try to be your own shepherd.

The former leads to peace.
The latter leads to a spiral.

Option 1 is usually our desire.

When the Lord is our shepherd . . .
God gives us purpose.
God guides our day.
We're off the hook for trying to save the world.

But option 2 is often our default setting. It's usually how we wake up. Left on autopilot, we put ourselves at the center throughout the day.

When we are our own shepherds . . .
It's our job to find purpose.
It's our job to come up with a plan for the day.
It's our job to fix everyone's problems.

One simple decision that leads to two dramatically different approaches to the day.

Here's my rendition of Psalm 23 when we get the first line wrong and fall for the trap of thinking we are our own shepherds.

I Am My Own Shepherd

I am my own shepherd, I better figure this out.
I never lie down in green pastures,
because I always feel like I'm running out of time.
I hope I'm on the right path
for my name's sake.
I try to avoid the darkest valley,
because I'm terrified of what I may find.
I know it's on me to protect myself,
and that gives me very little comfort.
I prepare my own table
but never sit down.
I try to manufacture enough energy
to get through the day,
because I'm on an endless search for goodness and love
all the days of my life,
and I will be searching for enough forever.

How do you feel? Anxious? Uptight? Truly uninspired? That's the unrelenting pressure of self-centeredness.

David wasn't called a man after God's own heart because he was perfect (he was far from it).[2] He was called a man after God's own heart because he truly believed the first line of this psalm: "The LORD is my shepherd, I lack nothing." He knew he was nothing without God. So to David, spirituality wasn't a way to affirm his own self-reliance; it was an invitation to surrender.

To think about the self *less.*
By thinking about God *more.*

Lord, free me from me.

Breath Prayer

Mornings can be brutal, but it can be incredibly helpful to start with breath. Let's be honest: Sometimes in the morning, breathing is about all you have to offer. But that's enough because each breath is an invitation to pray. A vehicle that takes you closer to God.

We'll be stopping sporadically throughout this book to practice breath prayer together. Here's my plea: Don't skip these. Imagine ordering a workout program, sitting in a coffee shop, and watching the explanation of the program every day, but never actually exercising. You can memorize all the commands, but if you don't put them into practice, you aren't going to get in shape.

Now for the game plan:

Spend a few minutes of every morning working through Psalm 23:1. When your alarm goes off and is followed quickly by your mind fixating on all the pressure you put on yourself, reverse the spiral. Instead, start each day by taking a humbling step of surrender to demote self and promote the Lord with breath prayer.

Inhale: The Lord is my shepherd.
Exhale: I lack nothing.

Inhale for five seconds.
Exhale for five seconds.
Do this five times.

As you go, you'll probably notice . . .
Round 1 is uncomfortable.

Round 2 is even more uncomfortable.
Round 3 helps you settle in a bit.
Round 4 is kind of nice.
Round 5 is when you actually start to believe you have a good shepherd who takes care of you.

Try it out right now. And then tomorrow morning, when all the pressure of being human pulls you out of your sleep, combat it with this breath prayer. Before you turn to your phone, before you reach for distractions, before you listen to the world's opinions about you, use your breath to remind your entire being about God's truth.

You have a shepherd.
You have all that you need.

He is the center of the story.
Not you.

Exhale and go enjoy your day.

Layer 2 | The Comparer

From Self-Righteousness to God's Righteousness

Truth Statement: ***I am created in the image of a self-sacrificial God.***

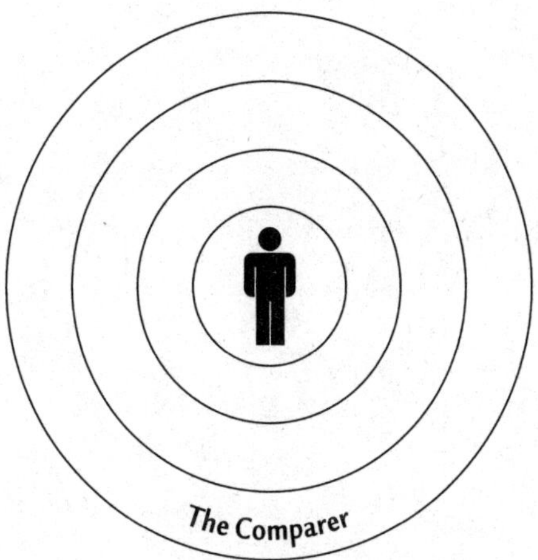

2.1: The Me-Maze (Part 2)

The Subway

Apparently, no one else had gotten the memo about the soul retreat in St. Patrick's Cathedral. With one step out of the sacred space, the silence became a distant memory. Horns were back to honking, store owners were back to shouting, and even more people seemed to be streaming down the sidewalk.

I walked a few blocks and spotted the staircase that descended into the wild underworld of New York City. It turned out, after all that, I was a quick walk away from the entrance I'd been searching for so dramatically (it's funny how, with the proper perspective, most of the things we stress about end up being no big deal).

I descended the first flight of stairs.
And then another.
Losing my sense
of direction
a bit more
with each
step.

I boarded my train and snagged the last open seat next to a massive man in a suit that barely fit him. His slicked-back black hair was almost as shiny as the gold tie caught over his left shoulder. He was on a business call. It wasn't going well. At least, that's what I gathered from the alarming number of words my publisher wouldn't let me put in this book. In most rooms, his tone alone would have raised alarm—but down in the subway, no one cared.

The man on the far side of the train had his entire life in his backpack. He was muttering words to himself on repeat loud enough for the rest of us to hear—talking to himself about himself, and the words weren't kind. In most rooms, everyone would have been on edge—but down there, no one cared.

I was still recovering from the mild panic attack that had led me to the cathedral and the paradigm-shifting experience that had left me feeling almost soothed. In most rooms, everyone would have wanted to hear the tale—but down there, no one cared.

The subway, I noted, is the great equalizer.

I took out my journal, trying not to interrupt the business negotiations going on next to me, and scribbled a note:

The businessman yelling at his phone.

The homeless man yelling at himself.

The burned-out pastor yelling internally.

We all have something in common.

It doesn't matter who you are. When self is at the center, you have to deal with the gravitational pull of life.

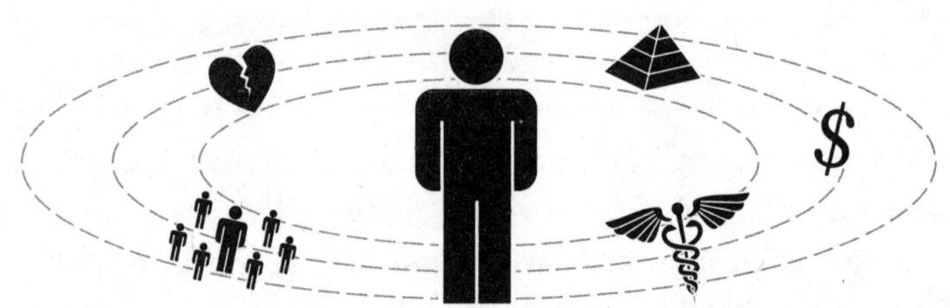

I closed my eyes and thought back to the very last undergraduate lecture I'd ever had as a psychology major at the University of Colorado.

"One last thing," my typically very stern professor had said as she set up her closing remarks. "We're all bozos on the same bus."

The class was confused. Some tried to write the line down, conditioned to still worry about exams even though we were graduating in a few days.

"Don't ever forget that," she said, cracking her first smile of the semester. "Pursue this career path, and you'll see just about every piece of brokenness in this world. Never make the mistake of thinking you're above it—like you know better."

We're all bozos on the same bus.

I've seen nothing but proof of that sentiment over the years.

Maybe it's easier for you to spot other people's problems than your own. Maybe you're an expert at identifying those who think too highly of themselves—the hard-driving businessman who thinks he owns the train. Or you jump to conclusions about those who think too lowly of themselves—the wanderer living in the train. But it's a lot harder to look in the mirror and remember you're on the train, too.

At my stop, I gladly jumped out and began to navigate out of the underground maze. As I went, I wondered how gold-tie guy's negotiations were going.

How do you get to a point where you think shouting obscene words into a phone in a public place is okay?

I thought about how mortified I'd be if I did that. And how I'd probably try to track everyone down and apologize multiple times. And how I was so much holier because I save my angry outbursts for when I'm alone and then try to convince everyone else I'm happy.

Comparison is a futile game when we're all bozos on the same bus.

Lord, free me from me.

And then there was the man at the end of the train, arguing with himself. I wondered how long he'd been there.

And if he had any family trying to find him.
And if he'd chosen that life or that life had chosen him.
And if he wanted something more.
And if he cared.
And if he knew something I didn't.

It's easy to jump to conclusions:

Well, I would never . . .
If they would just . . .

It's a lot harder to look in the mirror and realize I'm capable of the same level of delusion.

I wondered if that man on the subway was a messenger. A warning sign our judgments and preconceived notions wouldn't let us see. A picture of the extreme outworking of a mistake we were all making.

On my way to the final set of stairs, I passed half a dozen other humans who appeared to have made this subway station their home.

No doubt you pass the same kinds of people every day. Humans stuck in their own heads. Trapped in the me-maze. Each an individual soul with their own unique story.

For some, it's an addiction.
For some, it's an unlucky break.
For some, it's a mental health issue.
For some, it's a falling-out with family.
For all it's a complicated combination of several factors.

It's easy to walk by them and think, *I've got the solution. I'll buy you a cup of coffee and give you a five-step plan for how you can turn this all around in six weeks.*

But as anyone familiar with this arena can attest, it's not that simple. The me-maze has some deep, dark underground alleyways. More complex than the 665-mile New York City subway system. Places we can get to in our own inner world that are next to impossible to escape. Where some see a logical way out, others see a brick wall.

The me-maze is real.

This isn't a homeless problem; it's a human problem. The me-maze has no jurisdiction. It affects the rich just as much as the poor—the businessman, the beggar, and the burned-out pastor.

You are here, existing in this external world as you read this book. And at the same time, you are lost in your own inner world. A deep, dense labyrinth of beliefs (some true, some not), unprocessed pain, and all sorts of positive and negative memories that keep you stuck thinking about yourself.

So comparing ourselves with others or looking down on them and believing we know better than them is, at some tragic level, comical.

How often do we compare ourselves with versions of gold-tie guy only to realize that parts of us resonate with him? The puffed-up ego that thinks our problems are more important than everyone else's peaceful train ride? But we don't care. If we can just hustle more than others, improve faster than others, make more money than others, we'll know we have what it takes.

Other times we end up preaching to ourselves the same way the man at the back of the train was preaching to himself—loud, repetitive, and mean.

I thought about my panic attack earlier. I thought about how prone I am to turn spirituality into a performance and then compare my act with others. To this day, I'm still much better at preaching about peace than living peacefully.

Bozos on the same bus.

The sun was high in the sky as I ascended the final stair, only a short walk from the Morgan Library. My eyes took a moment to adjust as I scanned the area to get my bearings, suddenly all too aware of the next layer of the me-maze.

The Comparer.

Can you resonate with this second layer? When you fall into the trap of believing you're the center of the story, life becomes one giant competition. As though you can climb your way out of the hole if you can just move faster than others. But as we're about to find out, comparison only throws us deeper and deeper into the me-maze.

However, if you can learn to outsmart comparison by getting really good at spotting it and refusing to go any further, instead turning back and fixing your eyes on Jesus, the next layer of your me-maze will begin to crack. It'll get weaker, making your soul freer.

Chip.
Chip.
Chip.

But we've got a lot of work to do before we can get there. Starting with understanding how we fall into the comparison trap in the first place. I (re)learned that lesson the hard way, the week my first book became available for preorder.

2.2: The Comparison Trap

How We Get Caught Comparing

Today is the most important day of my life.

I finished my overly dramatic pep talk in the mirror and hit "publish" on the trailer for my first book, *Single Today.* It was finally available for preorder, and my journey to prove myself to the world had officially begun.

I love to write.
I want to keep writing.
So naturally, I wanted the book to do well.

Which is great.
And dangerous.

I had a whole team of amazing friends who were ready to help me spread the word. The trailer was going to be shared an annoying number of times. And hopefully, those shares would convert to book sales. And those book sales would convert to confidence for me.

Amazon has this lovely ranking feature that tells you how well your book is performing compared with every other book. I'd spent the last ten years writing in coffee shops, mostly words no one will ever see. But now I was getting thrown into the middle of the game, and thanks to Amazon, I could compare my success (or lack thereof) with every other writer I'd ever admired.

A perfectly dangerous drug for someone wired like me.

That morning, it was going well. And because of that, for the first time in a long time, I felt confident in my writing. And confident in myself.

I was still asking the same old questions: *Am I enough? Do I have what it takes?*

The only thing that had changed was my performance, which was centered on the book I'd been working so hard on.

Remember, **the Performer** is just the puppet dancing. The puppet master pulling the strings is **the Comparer.** And for me, **the Comparer** was running the part of me that didn't just want to put a good book out into the world but wanted said book to sell better than other books.

The Amazon ranking was my latest litmus test. If I climbed high enough, the answer (I'd convinced myself) would be a resounding "Yes, congratulations, Ryan. You are officially *enough.*"

I headed to the church and sat in my meetings, but I wasn't present. I googled how often Amazon updated the rankings: every hour on the hour. I stared at the clock, urging 11 A.M. to arrive like I'd once done in elementary school.

Back then, 11 A.M. meant recess, time to go outside and play basketball with my friends. That day, 11 A.M. meant **the Comparer** would get another review.

11 A.M. came around.
The review was staggering.
I fist-pumped in my office.
The Comparer took a bow.

At 3 P.M., the book had another spike. It climbed up the ranks so high that it was in the same category as a few of my heroes.

I took a screenshot.
Dopamine rushed into my brain.
It felt like bliss.

That night, I went to sleep happy.

The next morning was miserable. The book had been trending in the wrong direction since 5 A.M.

I'd been given my dream for a day. Then I had to watch Amazon slowly drag it away from me a little more every hour on the hour.

I went to work, but again, I wasn't present. Instead, I was googling how the rankings work. It turned out, selling a bunch of books isn't enough; it's about selling them *consistently.*

Day-of sales weigh the most.
The next day, they weigh only half.
And then half of that the next day.
And so on.

Hitting a bunch of sales quickly propelled me into an upper echelon I'd dreamed of being in. The problem was, now everyone I knew had already ordered their copy. It was all downhill from there.

Being ranked next to *Mere Christianity* was cool, until I remembered C. S. Lewis died sixty years ago. He hadn't had some flashy book trailer come out that week, and he was still outselling me from beyond the grave.

Whatever, Clive.

It was a cruel joke.
And my inner **Comparer** was devastated.

What should've been a joyful day was now packed full of pressure.

I'm sure you know the feeling. You've probably stepped into your fair share of comparison traps. So you know how good it can feel when it's working, and how devastating it can be when it's not.

How do you know if you have what it takes? If you are enough? Easy—you compare yourself with others. If you're trending in the right direction, all is well.

If you're trending in the right direction . . .

Lord, free me from me.

That evening, I sat on my back porch, rocking back and forth like a drug addict going through withdrawals. I tried breath prayer, but the pressure was unrelenting. I preordered a copy of my own book—then I felt like a fraud. **The Comparer** in me shook its head. Plus, it didn't even help the rank.

I was in a bad place.

The frustrating part was, I knew better. I really did. Even as I rocked back and forth on my back porch, I could laugh at myself. I could have stood up in that moment and preached a sermon about how silly the comparison game is because my identity is in Christ.

But the drug is real.

One part of me knew I was a child of God—created in God's image. But another part of me believed I was at the center of this story, in charge of being better than others to prove I had what it takes.

The new self might be content to reflect God's glory, but the old self is always trying to get its own glory.

And although the old self is gone and the new is here, that doesn't mean there aren't layers of residue to work through. Almost as though there are still plaques of the old self hanging on the wall.

Waiting.
Loitering.

And when the old self sees an opening, it tries to put itself back at the center. Spinning that tale we've talked about at length—the lie that the rest of the world revolves around you—to pull you right back into the me-maze.

I'd imagine you have your own form of this story.
Yours may not be quite so dramatic.
Then again, maybe it's way more dramatic.

Either way, welcome to the second role the old self loves to play: **the Comparer.**

Comparison

Comparers are constantly aware of the standings in every room they walk into—even when they have to make up their own metrics. I bet the part of you that compares has found its own ways to rank itself next to others.

Maybe for you . . .
The joy of romance becomes, *Wait—how old was that person when they got married? I better hurry up.*
The joy of a promotion becomes, *Wait—how much did that other employee get?*
The joy of raising children becomes, *Wait—their kid is already walking? And reading?*
The joy of saving up for a new home becomes, *Wait—theirs has a pool?*

There's a reason comparison is called "the thief of joy."[1] Comparison takes all the beauty of the world that is here for you to enjoy and turns it into a competition you will inevitably lose. Because the truth is, **the Comparer** has some really great days—but mostly tough ones.

The world can be kind to **the Comparer.** And the world can be incredibly cruel.

Sometimes your book rankings go up.
Other times they go down.

Sometimes you get the promotion.
Other times it goes to that co-worker in the next cubicle who clips their toenails during office hours.

Sometimes people laugh at your joke.
Other times they give all their attention to the "big humor, pie in the face" cheap-laugh guy you can't stand.

Sometimes you get a date.
Other times you get rejected and spend the night at home by yourself scrolling through social media only to discover that weird, awkward high school friend got engaged before you.

Whatever, Clive.

Insert your own experience here.

The point is, **the Comparer** will never be satisfied. A bump in your book sales will satisfy you for about three seconds.

This is incredible.

One, one thousand.
Two, one thousand.
Three, one thousand.

We have to climb higher.

It's never enough. And that's because there is a logical flaw in the comparison trap. A flaw that keeps everything (especially spirituality) about self.

The good news is, when you learn how to name that logical flaw, you can start knocking down this next wall in your maze.

2.3: The Logical Flaw of Comparison

How Comparison Inevitably Leads to Perfectionism

"I rolled," I shouted embarrassingly loud at the TV as my controller flew across the room. "I hit Y." The cord eventually tightened, snapping the controller back toward me. It didn't matter at that point; the speedrun was over.

And it wasn't user error (I'm convinced). The Super Nintendo I'd had since 1994 hadn't registered the button I pushed fast enough.

I'm not a gamer, but there is one game I grew up playing—*Donkey Kong Country* on Super Nintendo. I'm really good at it. I can beat the whole game in one sitting. Which opened my eyes to an entire subculture in the video-game world called speedruns, in which the goal is to finish the game as quickly as possible.

My record was 59 minutes.
Then after some practice I got down to 52 minutes.
And then 42 minutes.
And then, one fateful night when the stars aligned, I hit 38 minutes.

Preorders for my book had been available for the last month. I'd been doing my best to do two things—promote the book as much as I could and avoid obsessing over the ranking.

I was managing the former.
I was failing in the latter.

Early mornings were spent creating content to promote the book before I went to my day job (the church). Then I'd get home feeling exhilarated but exhausted, looking for a way to not think about anything for an hour. I'd made the executive decision that *Donkey Kong* speedruns would be my hobby.

And it was really fun until I googled the fastest way around a particular level and stumbled onto a YouTube video of some gamer named tjp7154 doing a speedrun in 31 minutes.

Remember, a few nights earlier I'd gotten 38 minutes and been ecstatic. But suddenly I couldn't stop thinking about 31.

Here's the problem: 31 is insane.
Go watch it on YouTube.
Every move is nearly perfect.

In the game, you can kill an enemy by jumping on them or rolling through them. Whenever you roll through them, you gain speed.

So while conventional wisdom says to avoid the enemies . . .
Speedrunners seek them out for the speed boost.

(What's this book about, again?)

In order to do a speedrun in 31 minutes, you have to roll through every enemy perfectly—it's truly impressive.

But it left me in my office trying to do the same thing.
While the controller flew across the room.

This is supposed to be fun.
Why am I feeling so much pressure?

For a few weeks, speedruns had been a nice break—then they became stressful. Why? What happened? With one silly search on YouTube, I'd fallen into the comparison trap.

Personal records are fun to try to beat, because you're comparing yourself with your former self. But world records, on the other hand, are incredibly stressful to try to beat, since you're comparing yourself with the best in the world.

Whatever, tjp7154.

When we shoot for a personal record, the goal is progress.
When we shoot for the world record, the goal becomes perfection.

That is the logical problem with comparison. No matter how good you get at something, there's always going to be a tjp7154 out there who is better than you. Which means the comparison trap is always going to push you toward being a perfectionist. And I hate to tell you this, but you are far from perfect.

The comparison trap turns the pursuit of progress into an obsession with perfection. And there's a massive difference between the two—both in *Donkey Kong* and in life.

First, *Donkey Kong*

When you're shooting for progress, a speedrun is exhilarating. You hit a new shortcut and come alive. As you play, you can tell you're ahead of your last record, so the further along you get, the more exciting it becomes.

But when you're shooting for perfection, a speedrun is nerve racking. Each moment, you're waiting for the other shoe to drop, so the further along you get, the more terrifying it becomes—the pressure is palpable.

And when you mess up, you throw your controller across the room.

Now, Life

In the beginning, the Creator of the universe began creating. Light, land, water, trees, animals, people. At the end of each creation, the text tells us, "God saw that it was good."[1] The Hebrew word for "good" is *tov*, which means "beautiful, desirable, agreeable, functional, life-giving."[2] What it doesn't mean is "perfect."

If God made everything perfect and then put man in the garden, the commission would be, "Don't ruin it." We would be like kids walking through a china shop, trying not to breathe too hard.

Thankfully, that's not the case. Even before the Fall, we were a work in progress. So why do you, in your broken, sinful state, hold yourself to the standard of perfection? The most basic answer is that perfectionism is the logical conclusion of comparison.

There is always going to be someone better than you.
There will always be someone smarter.
There will always be someone prettier.
There will always be someone funnier.

Only one person can come out of the comparison trap on top, and they will always be in danger of losing the throne. That's an awful lot of pressure.

And few things breed comparison faster than spirituality.

Spirituality and Comparison

Think about some of the spiritual practices.

Giving.
Serving.
Praying.

Spiritual practices are designed to help you reorient yourself to a Christ-centered spirituality. But then comparison sneaks in and flips it.

Take serving, for example. When you serve others, you experience the freedom found in getting your eyes off yourself. And then the next week, you do it again. But the third time, you might reach a point when you can't help but notice that you are better at serving than that other person. And when they get some praise for something you did, you grow a bit bitter. So you decide to double up on the hours you serve, because you don't want to fall behind in the made-up rankings the comparison trap created. Before you know it, you're thinking about yourself again. Except this time, it's harder to see, because you're doing it in the name of serving. Then you put a bunch of pressure on it. You've made serving others all about you.

That can happen with any of the practices.

Prayer can become about being more dedicated than others.
Fasting can become about being tougher than others.
Giving can become about trusting God more than others.

Comparison turns helpful ways to connect with God into competitions that throw us back into the me-maze.

Lord, free us from us.

Maybe that's why some of the harshest critiques and sharpest debates are about spiritual matters. You humbly set out to learn something about the infinite God this whole story gravitates around. Then you help someone else understand it, and they validate you for that.

And then you start looking for other people to teach it to.
Then you start noticing people who don't understand it.
Then you start judging them.
Then you start critiquing them.
Then you start publicly critiquing them.

And before you know it, your work has stopped being about God and now it's about trying to show the world that you are smarter than other people.

To use Paul's language, "Knowledge puffs up."[3]

Not to compare traps, but comparison may be the most dangerous in all of spirituality. It seamlessly finds ways to take good things and make them about you.

When you're doing well, you feel really good about yourself because you feel like you're moving up in the ranks. So, you get on a subway train and immediately start judging the loud, obnoxious businessman in the gold tie or the homeless guy at the other end.

Worse, when you mess up, you feel doubly bad about yourself because you feel like you're falling behind. And that's when things start to get weird, because that's when we are prone to take matters into our own hands with all the religious games we play.

Comparison throws us into the center of the story, so we strive for perfection. And when we don't hit it, we look for ways to make up for our imperfections. The theological word for this is *atonement.* In which we try to do a bunch of things in our own strength to make up for our shortcomings.

We've reached a pivotal point in this journey. If you can understand God-centered atonement versus self-centered atonement, comparison will begin to look really silly and the next wall in the me-maze will come crashing down.

Let's turn there next.

2.4: Atonement

Why Spiritual Score Keeping Is Silly

The crisp morning breeze whipped across my face, pushing me back toward my house—and my warm bed. Boulder, Colorado, is always beautiful, but when a gentle layer of snow covers the tops of the Flatirons, it's in the running for one of the most breathtaking places on earth.

On that morning, though, I couldn't have cared less. I was just angry it was September and already cold. I stared at the hills, but I couldn't appreciate them. I was too livid to really look. Livid not with others but with myself.

Stop partying.

That was my motto after that transformative summer of mission work. Now I was back in Boulder, feeling caught between two worlds—the sacred and the secular.

The freedom I'd felt all summer serving others.
And the bondage I felt at the number one party school in America.

The former felt like work but led to freedom.
The latter felt like fun but led to bondage.

I was trying hard to change, but the struggle was real. I'd be good for a few weeks, and then I'd have a night like last night.

Five bags.

Instead of attempting to lead more worship nights in my living room, I'd shifted my focus to starting an outreach in which we packed brown bags with socks, snacks, and water to give to people on the streets. The homeless population is extensive in Boulder, and I wanted to make sure we had some tangible way to help. "Bonus points," I'd always say, "if it leads to learning their name and getting into a conversation."

But conversations weren't my goal that morning. I was just trying to balance the scales. Five bags was my self-inflicted punishment for a night of debauchery. So although my body desperately needed sleep, my mind needed something else—atonement.

Five bags. Then back to bed.

A few blocks in, I met a guy named Dustin. He told me he had been trying to get sober but had relapsed the night before.

Externally, I nodded.

Internally, I compared his night with mine to make myself feel better. (Because, you know, my moral lapse was somehow less bad than his.)

He could tell I wasn't in the mood to talk. He thanked me for the brown bag, and we went our separate ways. I figured that would be the last time we'd meet, but that ended up being far from true.

An hour later, I trekked back up to my college house, hoping someone from church had seen me out there braving the cold like the saint I was. By then, the sun was fully risen in the eastern sky, thawing out my empty hands. Somewhere behind me, five people down on Pearl Street had some warm socks and a few snacks to get their day started.

Great.

That truth, like the snowcapped hills, was a beauty I couldn't see.

All I could think about was that I'd made a mistake.
I knew I had to atone.

Not because of a Bible verse.
Not because of an accountability group.
Not because of some weird church rule.

But because I was keeping score. It's like I'd created a spiritual hierarchy in my mind, where all of us college kids were trying our best to follow God, and I was keeping track. The night before, I'd fallen behind compared with the kids who hadn't partied, and I'd woken up determined to climb back up the ranks.

The unrelenting pressure of trying to control spirituality on my own terms was driving my life.

Five bags. Are we good, God?

Self-Righteousness

Humans have been trying to atone for our shortcomings since that notorious bite out of the fruit, when Adam and Eve started believing that the loving Creator going for a walk in the coolness of the day was actually a cosmic police officer out on patrol.

Remember that performance we talked about in part 1? With the questionable costume design (fig leaves) and the bad reviews? Their performance was an attempt to atone for their sin. As was my hungover morning outreach on Pearl Street.

I'd imagine you have your own version of *five bags.*

I shouldn't have made that joke, but I'll sprinkle in three compliments to that person I offended today.

I shouldn't have gone back to that vice, but after two days of sobriety, I'll tell my group about it.
That business deal was shady, but I'll give 10 percent of the proceeds to a non-profit.

Whatever your modus operandi, the heart is the same—make up the ground your mistake caused you to lose.

Trying to make up for our shortcomings with good behavior is the natural outworking of a self-centered focus. After all, you are the one who got yourself into this mess; you'd better get yourself out. At some level, that's the logic behind every other major world religion. Except there's a massive problem with that logic.

Because while I was trying to atone for my sins by passing out five bags, I was judging the people I gave them to, hoping someone from the church would see me being "spiritual," and ultimately doing all of this because I was comparing my righteousness with my friends'.

In other words, even while I was trying to pay off my debt, I was accruing more.

You see the problem, right? And the unrelenting pressure self-centeredness creates? We'll never be able to atone on our own, because we don't just sin; we are *sinners*. So, we don't just need some good behavior; we need a Savior.

Fortunately, we have one.

The apostle John once wrote, "This is love: not that we loved God, but that he loved us and sent his Son as an *atoning sacrifice* for our sins. Dear friends, since God so loved us, we also ought to love one another."[1] The key to loving others is first realizing that Jesus is our *atoning sacrifice*.

I'm going to guess you didn't use that phrase in your vernacular today, so a quick note on both words.

Atonement

The English word *atonement* originally meant "at-one-ment." It's the reconciling of two parties. One party wrongs the other and creates separation. But then they do something to make up for it—to *atone* for their behavior—and the two parties are brought back together.

So *atonement* is a decent English word, but the Hebrew word for "atonement" that John would've grown up hearing has another layer to it—the word is *kippur. Kippur* is an essential theme all throughout Scripture. It comes from a word that means "to cover."[2] It doesn't just pay the debt; it also purifies (or covers) the party involved.

Imagine being a convicted felon in prison. It would be one thing if the warden came to your cell and said, "You've been forgiven; you can go." That would be great, but you'd still be a convicted felon who is going to have an uphill battle to get your life back on track.

Kippur is getting at something more. It would be more like the warden telling you, "You're free to go, your record has been expunged, and you're being given a medal that is going to open up all sorts of doors for you."

You're covered—that's much better news.

So John calling Jesus the "atoning sacrifice for our sins" is him saying, "Jesus covered it. He didn't just forgive us; he made it right. How can he do that? Because of his sacrifice."

Sacrifice

Our choices bring death to this world. Or as Paul said, "The wages of sin is death."[3]

In the Old Testament, atonement was made through animal sacrifice. The book of Leviticus lays out a number of rules and methods for sacrifices throughout the year. And then there was one day a year called "the Day of Atonement" (Yom Kippur) when the high priest took two goats, sacrificed one, and then put both his hands on the head of the second, confessed all the sins of the people, and sent this scapegoat into the wilderness. Together, those two goats atoned for (covered) the sins of the people for the year.[4]

But of course, people kept sinning, and the system had to continue.

Enter Jesus.

The writer of Hebrews said it better than I ever could: "Unlike the other high priests, he [Jesus] does not need to offer sacrifices day after day, first for his own sins, and then for the sins of the people. He sacrificed for their sins once for all when he offered himself."[5]

The sacrificial system was never-ending. The only way out of the unrelenting pressure was someone coming in and making the perfect sacrifice. That's what Jesus did. He laid down his life to cover our sins once and for all. He took the wrath we deserve, drinking the cup for us so that we could go free.

Paul summed it up well: "God made him who had no sin to be sin for us, so that in him we might become the righteousness of God."[6]

Via his sacrifice, Jesus covers us. We are now the righteousness of God.

Imagine we went to dinner together and you picked up the tab. But then I sneaked back in a few minutes later and tried to pay it again myself. The hostess would probably look at me in confusion, thinking back to her training, which never covered a preposterous situation like this. Eventually she'd look at me and say, "Why are you trying to pay for a tab that's already been covered?"

Jesus is our *atoning sacrifice.*
Which is why self-centered spirituality leads to pressure.
But Christ-centered spirituality leads to peace.

You are covered . . .
Not because you passed out five bags to people on the street.
Not because you shared your faith with your co-worker.
Not because you gave 10 percent.

All those things are great, but they don't give you right standing in front of God. If they did, righteousness would be on you—self-righteousness.

That's reason 985 that it's a good thing God is at the center of this whole thing. Jesus freed you from you.

When we believe the lie that we are at the center of the story, atonement is on our shoulders—so all of us are trying to do a lot of really good things to try to right our wrongs, and we're all exhausted.

And then Jesus says things like, "Come to me, all you who are weary and burdened, and I will give you rest,"[7] and it sounds like a foreign language.

Rest? Sounds good in theory, Jesus. But ever since I dipped my toe in this whole spirituality thing, I'm mostly just worn out and overwhelmed.

Exhaustion will always be the fruit of trying to build the kingdom without the King. Because you'll constantly be plagued with the question, *How much is enough?*

Even if my logic had been correct regarding handing out bags to tip the scales, I would be left with an impossible question to answer.

How many bags are enough?

Handing out five bags to people on the street doesn't make us righteous, but what about five hundred? Or how about five thousand?

Think about it: If righteousness was on me, then there would have to be a number. What would it be?

Fifty thousand?
Five million?

There's got to be a number, right? It was just one night of partying.

You may hear that and think it's an absurd question. But it's the logical outworking of so many people's approaches to spirituality.

Instead, we get to experience the deep soul rest of knowing that Christ, the one in charge, is our atoning sacrifice. You are being transformed into the image of a self-sacrificial God. And the fact that Jesus covers the bill means that any sort of spiritual scorekeeping can go out the window.

Comparing your goodness to others' goodness . . .
And your badness to others' badness . . .
Is all a silly waste of time.

And with that theology as our foundation, we are ready to get really practical and talk about the two words that will break you out of the comparison trap and free you from you: *in Christ.*

2.5: In Christ

The Simple Phrase That Destroys Comparison

Blink-182 blasted through the speakers of my Chevy Cruze as I slowly made my way to church. The song reminded me of simpler times, back before all the pressure and expectations—before I was a "pastor." No one else was putting quotes around that word, just me.

I am a pastor.
I have the paperwork to prove it.
I just didn't feel like one on that particular day—hadn't all week.

Pastors are supposed to be super spiritual. They're supposed to pray without ceasing and never cuss, but I hadn't managed to do either of those things that week.

I turned my music down as I entered the church parking lot and put on a spiritual podcast in case someone got in my car after church.

Wow, Ryan listens to some really deep stuff.

Earlier that week, a friend of mine had sent me a sermon from a guy I respected who had preached a similar sermon to one I had just given . . . but his was way better. And it made me want to quit. And then when I reasoned that his was better because he was older than me, I made the mistake of going back to a sermon he had preached when he was my age. It turns out, he was better back then, too. And then I really wanted to quit.

The first song began, and I slipped into the back of the auditorium.

A guest speaker named Mike took the stage with a series of self-deprecating jokes that immediately won me over. His sermon was about how Ephesians can be broken into two parts.

Ephesians 1–3 is all about who we are in Christ.
Ephesians 4–6 is all about how we should act in light of it.

Theologians often call it the indicative and the imperative.
The indicative is what God has done for us.
The imperative is what we should do in response.

Ephesians 1–3: the indicative (what Jesus has done for us).
Ephesians 4–6: the imperative (what we should do in response).

Mike was driving home the point that Paul never flipped that order. He always reminded us who we are in Christ before he invited us to live into that calling. Which is important because when we forget chapters 1–3, we turn all the action steps in 4–6 into a list of chores and then heap shame on ourselves when we fall short.

"I got married at twenty-nine," Mike explained. "From eighteen to twenty-nine, I lived on my own, and during those eleven years, I lived a lifestyle fitting for a bachelor."

The room started laughing, predicting where he was going.

"I had three piles of laundry—clean, worn once, and unclean—and then when three piles became one pile, I knew it was time to do laundry."

I thought about the three piles of clothes in my room and nodded, appreciating the efficiency of his strategy.

Everyone else laughed.

I wasn't sure why.

"I lived in a manner congruent with being a single guy."

Mike then explained how he met his wife, fell in love, proposed, and stood in front of a pastor who pronounced them husband and wife.

"Was I a husband in that moment?" he asked rhetorically. "Yes, I have a certificate that says I'm married. But did I have any idea what it meant to be a husband? No, not even remotely."

The room laughed.

I was silent.

"The rest of my married life is about learning to become what is already true," he continued, talking right to me. "There were ways of speaking, acting, and living that were fitting for me as a bachelor but not as a husband. And so, I take those off and I put on those ways of speaking, acting, and living that are appropriate now for being married."

I thought about that piece of paper I had that says I'm a pastor and how I had spent most of the week feeling unworthy of it because I hadn't measured up compared with another pastor's highlight reels.

"And here's what's really important," Mike said, reining our attention back in. "I don't do all those things in order to become a husband. I do them because I already am a husband. Do you see the difference?"

I hadn't for the first twenty-five years of my life.

But as he spoke, I began to.

"Do you think I've got husbanding down yet?" he asked, landing the plane. "No. But it is the security of my covenant relationship with my wife that gives me the grace to imperfectly learn to be what I already am."

And then he said the line that got me: "I was declared a husband and then invited to be one."

I thought about all the unworthiness I felt and how it was caused by a comparison game God never asked me to play.

"In Christ you've got it all already," he said. "So become who you already are."

Less of Me—More of You

A few minutes later, Mike pulled out an action figure and placed him in a mason jar. "This is what it's like in Christ," he explained. As he raised and lowered the jar, he pointed out that Captain America moved along with it because Captain America was in the jar.

It's a simple, profound illustration of what it means to be in Christ. He's our atoning sacrifice—we're covered.

When you make a mistake—you're covered in Christ.
When you say something mean—you're covered in Christ.
When you realize you've thought about yourself every minute since you woke up and lived the entire day in the me-maze—you're covered in Christ.

You're being renewed in the image of your Creator, and that is a long, drawn-out process. But remember, you're "in Christ," so as you grow, you're covered the whole time.

You may have a deep, tangled, confusing me-maze. But as God continues to chip away at the layers, you can rest, knowing that

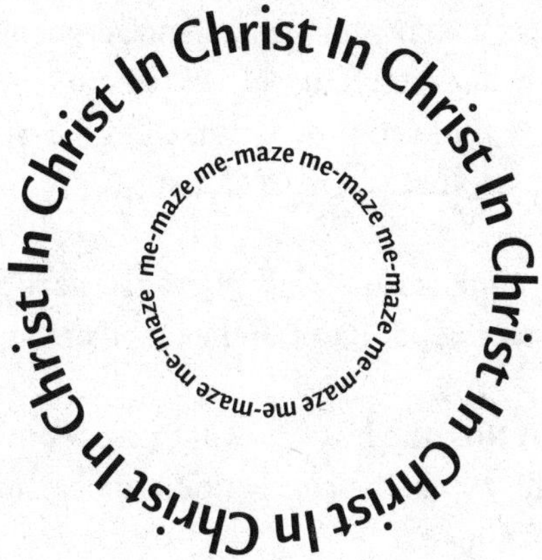

you're in Christ every step of the way. You don't have to work through a certain level of the me-maze to be in Christ. The whole point is that "while we were still sinners, Christ died for us."[1]

You're in Christ Jesus, which means your job is not to get it perfect but rather to reflect God's perfection the best you can.

Do you see why, in light of that truth, comparison is so silly?

When I get caught in the comparison trap with my writing and see my ranking start to fall, my flesh shouts at me, "Get to work." It tells me to earn my keep. To find a way to climb back up the ranks.

But in Christ . . .
Get to work . . .
Becomes *I get to work!*

I get to try to climb the ranks, not to prove anything to anyone, but because I believe in the things I'm writing and I might as well work to share them with as many people as possible.

I'm sure you have your own version of the comparison trap. Whether you're a lawyer, a nurse, a teacher, a stay-at-home parent, a therapist, a tech engineer, an entrepreneur, or a philanthropist—whenever your old self tries to tell you to get to work, to climb the ranks to prove yourself to the world, you can remind your old self that you're in Christ.

And "in Christ," comparison is silly. Because we're all *equally* in Christ. None of us can be "more in the jar" than anyone else.

The more you get this, the less you will think about yourself. Other people will stop being competition to beat and start becoming humans to love.

My friend Wade has a simple formula he tries to live by:

Less of me.
More of you.

When he feels himself falling into the comparison trap . . .

Less of me.
More of you.

When he just wants to check out after a long day of work but someone in his life needs a person to talk to . . .

Less of me.
More of you.

From the time they were young, he's taught his kids that those words are a cheat code for life, and it's worked. They are one of the most refreshing families to be around—a fun, life-giving group of people who care deeply about others and aren't caught in the maze of self-centeredness.

When you start to understand who you are in Christ, you can begin to do the same thing. God has work for us to do, and most of the time, that work involves serving, helping, and encouraging other people.

So before you rush off to the next chapter, take a moment and let this truth sink in by doing seven rounds of breath prayer with Ephesians 2:10:

> We are God's handiwork, created *in Christ Jesus* to do good works, which God prepared in advance for us to do.

Inhale: I am in Christ.
Exhale: God has work for me to do.

Inhale for five seconds.
Exhale for five seconds.
Do this seven times.

The comparison trap is nothing new. From the beginning, people have always been finding creative ways to twist spirituality into a competition. One of the most pertinent examples is an early heresy called Gnosticism. Let's go there next.

2.6: Gnosticism

The Not-So-Secret Knowledge and Why It Doesn't Work

"What if I told you that you can eat as much pizza as you want and still look like this?"

The YouTube ad popped up before the song I'd chosen as the soundtrack for my sermon prep. I tried to ignore it, but let's be honest: It was a pretty good opening line. I would in fact love to eat as much pizza as I wanted and still look like the guy on the video.

So I lingered.

The "skip" button popped up—YouTube deciding I'd paid my dues—but right before I could hit it, the guy told me to wait because his super-secret solution was both quick and easy. It turned out, I'd been lied to all these years. I don't know if you've heard, but fitness is actually quick and easy, and this guy had all the answers.

My sermon wasn't anywhere close to being done, but it was only Tuesday, so I heard him out. After all, he promised he was about to tell me the secret.

He didn't tell me.

Instead, he backed up and told me about his life and his own struggle to get in shape. Then three other people's stories. Then, right before he told me the secret, a link popped up, asking me to sign up to hear it.

I typically smell this type of stuff from a mile away, but I really love pizza, so I clicked. I put in my information, the more mature part of me shaking its head, while I imagined the guy watching from afar like Ursula convincing Ariel to give away her voice.

Then I got an email with another video of the guy talking for another five minutes until he finally made his big reveal. His super-secret solution was just his generic supplement line.

Are supplements helpful? Of course.
Are some better than others? Obviously.

But as I discovered, the person in the video wasn't eating as much pizza as he wanted. To look like him, you have to commit your life to an incredibly regimented routine (oh yeah, and often it's later revealed that steroids had something to do with it).

He was a salesman.
Using the comparison trap.
And I walked right into it.

I told myself to just skip the ad. It was the same week, and my sermon still wasn't close to being done. Except Tuesday had quickly become Friday and had me panicking.

A guy was sitting in his private jet, talking about money. Apparently, he'd once been broke. Apparently, he'd had multiple businesses fail. And apparently, his current one was foolproof.

He was going to give me his super-secret method for getting rich in his completely free webinar that would be available for only a small window of time to a select few—making me feel like Charlie finding the Golden Ticket.

I was just a guy trying to write a sermon.

I knew the salesman was full of it, but I also couldn't help but think he might have some super-secret formula. After all, the guy had a jet.

A lot of my friends are really passionate about health. Some are nutritionists; some are personal trainers; others just value living a full, vibrant life.

Whenever I ask them about those fit guys saying they have the secret knowledge that is going to change everything, they roll their eyes and say the same thing: *There's a way to get healthy, but it's not by taking a secret supplement. It's by eating right, exercising, and taking care of yourself.*

The problem is, that regimen doesn't sell quite as well.

I have friends in the finance world. They're passionate about helping people get out of debt, make good financial decisions, and build wealth.

Whenever I ask them about those finance gurus in their private jets, they roll their eyes and say the same thing: *There's a way to acquire wealth, but it's not a secret. It's by getting out of debt, making smart decisions, and playing the long game.*

The problem is, that advice doesn't sell quite as well.

I say all that to say this . . .
As a pastor, that's how I feel anytime I see someone peddling super-secret spirituality.

Manifest anything in twenty-one days.

You won't believe how fast this works.
Let me show you the super-secret way to get what you want.

Here's the thing: There's a way to experience a full, abundant life. Spirituality really does work. But guess what? It's not a secret. It's about following the way of Jesus laid out in Scripture.

It's about consistency and humility.

The problem is, that way of life doesn't sell quite as well. We're all busy. And stuck in the comparison trap. We don't have time for consistency; we need results in the next twenty-one days.

Especially if you've tried everything.
And you still can't seem to get that breakthrough.
And you still don't like your job.
And you still can't get that one person's attention.

You can see why super-secret self-centered spirituality sounds a lot better for that person in that moment, right?

You've been lied to.
Here's what they don't want you to know.
This actually works.
It's easier than you think.

Are those things actually what's best for you? Who cares? You want them. And you want them *now*—so you click.

And you take the course.
And you write out the statements.
And it kind of works at first.
And then you double down and attend a seminar.

And then six months later, you feel more lost and alone and confused than you did at first.

So you find your next guru.
And attend another seminar.
And pay more money.
And dive deeper into a self-centered spirituality that promises freedom but leads to bondage.
Welcome to the me-maze.

And the truth is, as long as you don't care about people, it's a brilliant marketing ploy. Because it hits a pain point. The "super-secret supplement" guy speaks to the person struggling to get in shape. The "pay me money and I will help you get rich" guy resonates with the person who has always struggled to get their finances in order. And the "you've been lied to—let me tell you how to manifest anything you want" guru hits a pain point with the person who can't seem to make spirituality work for them.

So again, brilliant marketing.
If you don't care about people.

Individuals and groups have been peddling *secret knowledge* forever.

It's been the go-to lie ever since the serpent whispered those fateful words in the garden: *You can be like God.*

The early church had their own version of the "super-secret knowledge they don't want you to know" crew.

We call them the Gnostics.

The Gnostics

Gnosticism was an early-church heresy popular in the second and third centuries. It comes from the Greek word *gnosis* meaning "knowledge." And the basic idea is that although we all have a spark of the divine in us, we are trapped here in our physical bodies.

Spirit = Good
Body = Bad

So, then, the goal of spirituality is the flight of the soul out of the physical and into the spiritual—ascending higher to be like God.

How do you ascend? Well, you need the gnosis, the special knowledge that'll help you break out of the material world and ascend into the spiritual.

Imagine having a conversation with someone who is down on their luck, keeps messing up, and can't seem to figure out spirituality. "Hey," you might say to that person, "you know how you keep doing the thing you don't want to do? There's a reason for that. You just haven't ascended high enough yet. It's not your fault; you never knew all the secrets."

(If you know your history, this has obvious influence from Plato, the famous Greek philosopher who said similar things around 400 B.C. And if you're even further ahead of me, yes. This way of thinking has returned with new age. After all, there's nothing new under the sun.)

Jesus and his disciples lived in the first century. Matthew, Mark, Luke, and John all wrote their gospels in the first century. But then, starting in the second century, several Gnostic texts began appearing.

The Secret Book of John.
The Gospel of Judas.
The Gospel of Thomas.
The Gospel of Mary Magdalene.

The dating is important here, because notice all those Gnostic texts claim to be written by original disciples. The problem is, they were written way after those original disciples were dead.

Meaning the Gnostics would come up with these new books containing "secret knowledge" and then pretend like it came from original disciples.

Brilliant marketing—if you don't care about people.

Around A.D. 180, a church father named Irenaeus gathered all the writings he could from Gnosticism (and other heresies) and put together a five-volume work called *Against Heresies.* In it, he wrote at length against Gnosticism: "These men falsify the oracles of God, and prove themselves evil interpreters of the good word of revelation. They also overthrow the faith of many, by drawing them away, under a pretense of [superior] knowledge."[1]

They peddled "superior knowledge" that ultimately led to the unrelenting pressure of a spirituality that started with the self.

Not all the Gnostic texts we have today were around by the time Irenaeus wrote *Against Heresies,* but it's clear he was referring to at least two—*The Gospel of Judas* and *The Secret Book of John.*

The Gospel of Judas is a wild ride about Judas collaborating with Jesus.

The Secret Book of John basically retells the Genesis account in a complicated new myth that illuminates something really important about Gnostics and new age. I'll give you the basics, and then you can go take a deeper dive on your own.

The Secret Book of John is a story about John the apostle. One day on his way to the temple, he had a concerning interaction with a Pharisee who told him Jesus had deceived him. John left in distress, headed out to the mountains, and started praying to know the real Jesus. And then Christ appeared (in three different forms) and gave John all this secret knowledge about what really happened.

Essentially, John learned that the god in Genesis wasn't the true, ultimate God. Instead, he was a lower (and evil) god named Yaldabaoth. He was the one who created the world and everything we see. (Remember, the Gnostics believed the material world wasn't all that great and was more like a prison our spirits were stuck in.)

Yaldabaoth didn't want humans to eat from the tree of the knowledge of good and evil, because he was a jealous god who didn't want us to know how powerful we are. He didn't want us to gain true spiritual knowledge (gnosis). So, the command to not eat the fruit wasn't to protect us; it was to protect himself.

Then the serpent (who actually appeared as an eagle in this story) came in as the ally to show us the way—to "raise them up from sleep's depths." Adam and Eve ate from the tree, their eyes were opened, and Yaldabaoth was furious.[2]

That's a very different story from the one we talked about in part 1, right? Remember how we talked about Adam and Eve trading in God-centered spirituality for self-centered spirituality and immediately feeling the pressure that caused them to sew fig leaves and hide?

The Gnostics would say that was the day they stumbled upon the secret knowledge that set them free.

Okay, put on your critical thinking cap and see if you can discern the major difference between the two stories. If you said, "Gee, Ryan, it kinda seems like these two stories illustrate the haunting difference between God-centered spirituality and self-centered spirituality," you hit the nail on the head.

Do you believe that God is at the center of this whole thing and that life works best when we humbly trust his way? Or do you believe that the gods and the church have been suppressing some secret knowledge about your own divinity?

Genesis tells the story of the former.
The Gnostics tell the story of the latter.

One requires surrender but leads to freedom.
The other promises freedom but leads to bondage.

From the very beginning, people have been coming up with creative ways to justify eating the fruit. When it comes to finding ways to satiate our burning appetite to be like God, we are incredibly creative: "Oh, spirituality hasn't been working for you? That's because you've been lied to. This is all about the secret knowledge that I have and that you need, so buy my overpriced course, and I'll tell you all about it. And by the way, did you know you can eat as much pizza as you want and still have no body fat?"

One last book to mention: *The Gospel of Thomas.*

The Gospel of Thomas

In 1945, a collection of (mostly Gnostic) manuscripts was discovered near Nag Hammadi. One of them (which has probably become the most famous Gnostic text) was *The Gospel of Thomas.*

When you hear a spiritual teacher quoting Jesus in a way you don't remember hearing in the Gospels, there's a good chance it's coming from *The Gospel of Thomas.* This series of 114 supposed sayings of Jesus was written in the second century (long after Thomas was gone). There is almost no narrative, just sayings (similar to the book of Proverbs). And the emphasis is on self-realization. Meaning, rather than salvation being found in Jesus as our *atoning sacrifice,* it's found in you. And once you properly understand the secret sayings of Jesus, you'll begin to wake up to this salvation.

Here's the prologue: "These are the hidden sayings that the living Jesus spoke and Didymos Judas Thomas wrote down."[3] Notice the secret-knowledge language right off the bat. And then it starts into the 114 sayings.

It's an interesting read. Some of it parallels the Gospels, some makes the subtle shift toward self-centered spirituality, and then some is downright absurd.

One of the most famous lines, saying 70, sums up the thread of the whole book well: "If you bring forth what is within you, what you have will save you. If you do not have that within you, what you do not have within you [will] kill you."[4]

Salvation is found within you, so bring it forth, or else it will destroy you. That is the anthem of spirituality that starts with the self. It's why spirituality can so easily downshift into self-discovery. And I get the appeal, but honestly—these days, that just sounds like an awful lot of pressure.

I have to bring it forth?
I have to save myself?
And if I don't, it'll kill me?

Most days, I can't even find my car keys.

Thank God that Jesus gives a different invitation: "Come to me, all you who are weary and burdened, and I will give you rest."[5]

Again, this book is a basic introduction to how we depend on the self to figure out all the answers of life and spirituality. Explaining Gnosticism in a single chapter is a fool's errand, but my hope is to get you thinking. There are lots of great resources out there to learn more.[6] But the point is, you can see why Gnosticism was so appealing back then. And why it keeps showing back up today.

Bishop Robert Barron calls Gnosticism "the most enduring heresy."[7] Because it just keeps coming back up. Today it takes the form of YouTube thumbnails:

You've been lied to.
They've been holding out on you.
I'll tell you what they don't want you to know.

Followers of Jesus have always been met with two options:

Option 1: Put Jesus at the center, where spirituality becomes about participating in the redemption and restoration of heaven and earth (the gospel).
Option 2: Put self at the center and make spirituality all about your own self-discovery.

When Jesus is at the center, you can take your place as an image bearer, ready to play your part in this much bigger story. When self is at the center, everything comes down to how you are feeling and how you are doing on any given day.

But life with Jesus is so much bigger than that. You are part of this bigger story. It's the story of God loving this world and the story of redemption and restoration. It's the story of the King of kings and his kingdom. And it's the story about how you are an image bearer, here to participate.

It's not a story about you discovering who you really are and becoming a god.
That story is too small.
And it puts way too much pressure on you.

Self-centered spirituality drives you deeper into the self.
Christ-centered spirituality sets you free from the self.

You're not divine. . . . Exhale.

We aren't created to be at the center. And when we try, we lose our humanness. But remember, the Holy Spirit is the re-humanizing Spirit who is in the process of restoring us.

Christianity Has a Marketing Problem

Gnosticism is only the beginning. The church has had to deal with two thousand years of heresies.

One of the red flags to always watch out for is the super-secret-knowledge ploy that plays into the comparison trap by promising to teach you how to get to special places other people don't understand.

The truth is, true Christian spirituality has a marketing problem. Because Jesus cared deeply about people. He was trying to help them, not sell them something. So, he said things like . . .

> Whoever wants to save their life will lose it, but whoever loses their life for me will find it.[8]
>
> Anyone who wants to be first must be the very last, and the servant of all.[9]
>
> Whoever wants to be my disciple must deny themselves and take up their cross daily and follow me.[10]

Do you see how different Jesus's version of spirituality is?
Significantly less marketable.
Infinitely more meaningful.

The longer I study spirituality, the less logical statements like "All paths lead to the same place" become. Take these two statements:

"Take up your cross and follow me."
"Manifest whatever you want five times faster."

Maybe I'm just not enlightened enough to see it, but I can't figure out how both of those strategies lead to the same place. It feels more like the former is an invitation to get out of the center of the story and the latter is a call to double down on self-centeredness.

But I digress.

The super-secret-knowledge ploy is almost always a creative way to teach people how to be divine. In other words, it allows you to keep self at the center. After all, *if you eat this fruit, you can be like God.*

But spirituality takes more than a super-secret supplement. There aren't passcodes or spells that'll magically take you to greater heights than other people so you can win some spiritual contest **the Comparer** is playing. Instead, there is a good God on the throne who loves you, created you to be his image bearer, and has a plan for your life.

The more you fix your eyes on God . . .
The more you devote your life to God . . .
The more you worship God . . .
The more you discover the beauty of repentance . . .
And the more grateful you become for the life God's given you . . .

The more the unrelenting pressure of self-centeredness will lose its power over your life.

Lord, free us from us.

Chip.
Chip.
Chip.

And that brings us to our final topic that leads to comparison: manifesting.

2.7: Manifesting

From Manifesting to Intercession

I sat in my backyard again, hitting the refresh button as I stared at my book ranking like Gollum in *The Lord of the Rings*.

It was late.
And I was stuck in the comparison trap.

I was trying to write some blog for some website that would hopefully push more people toward the book. But it wasn't flowing. I couldn't figure out what I wanted to say.

Probably because I couldn't stop checking my ranking, comparing how my book was doing against all the other authors in the world. The ones who were better than me. Who wouldn't struggle to write a simple blog.

A song by Elevation Worship called "The Blessing" was blaring in my headphones on repeat; it was the only thing keeping me sane.

I was stuck in the me-maze.
Worrying my book wouldn't be good enough.
Worrying it wouldn't sell.
Worrying I didn't measure up.

I was getting desperate and was ready to try anything. Anything, except figuring out how to end this blog. Instead, I was scrolling through YouTube, looking for another convenient distraction, when I saw it:

MANIFEST WHATEVER YOU WANT IN 48 HOURS—THIS REALLY WORKS

Like most online guided manifesting videos, the title spoke directly to my pain point: *Maybe I could manifest a bestselling book?*

I hovered over the video for a moment.

Should I do this?
Is it biblical?
What's the difference between this and prayer?

I get asked that question all the time. So, before I tell you if I clicked on the link, here are a few thoughts on manifesting.

The Good and the Bad

Even if you've never looked into it, you've probably heard about the concept of manifesting. It's based on the law of attraction—that you are attracting everything in your life through your thoughts and feelings. The popular quip is "Your personality creates your personal reality."[1]

Basically, you become and attract what you think about most. Which means, if you get really clear about what you want and really intentional about changing your thoughts and feelings to align with it, those things will manifest themselves in your life. Which, at a logical level, makes complete sense.

Take all the spirituality out of it for a second. The gurus in those videos who are teaching you how to manifest anything you want are doing two things really well.

The first is *goal clarity.*

Their whole point is that you have to see what you want before you can have it. And in order to see what you want, you have to *know* what you want. And humans are amazingly bad at knowing what we want. I wonder if that's why Jesus kept trying to get us to clarify our goals.

Think of Jesus asking the blind beggar, "What do you want me to do for you?"[2]

We all know the answer. The guy wanted to see. But Jesus was letting him say it out loud. "Rabbi, I want to see," he said, passing the test with flying colors.[3]

To which Jesus wildly responded, "Go, your faith has healed you."[4]

Something changes in us when we get crystal clear on our goals. Which brings up a good question: *Do you know what you want?*

Not your polite answer.
Not your super-spiritual answer.

Do you know what you actually want in life? What gets you out of bed in the morning?

We Christians love vague goals. Because vague goals let us get away with vague prayers, in which we loosely define what we think we kind of want (if it's God's will) so we don't have to be disappointed if it doesn't happen. Oftentimes, what we call humility is actually a lack of faith.

We could learn some things from the manifesting community about goal clarity.

The second thing they could teach us a thing or two about is the power of our thoughts. Thoughts are incredibly powerful. That's not a secular idea; it's Scripture. In one of the most quoted but least practiced verses of all time, Paul said, "Do not conform to the pattern of this world, but be transformed *by the renewing of your mind.*"[5]

The goal of this book is to be transformed into the image of Christ, and according to Paul, that process starts by renewing our minds. By thinking about what we think about.

At some level, the manifesting community seems to get that more than most Christians. And we should learn from them—because they are really just catching up with what Paul said two thousand years ago. Our thoughts drive feelings, feelings determine actions, and actions lead to results (for better or worse). So, new thoughts (a renewed mind) will lead to transformation.

But then there's the not-so-good side of manifesting: namely, that it becomes a cheaper, depersonalized version of God's beautiful design for prayer.

Prayer is communion with God—talking, listening, and sometimes just being still in his presence. It's the spiritual discipline we enter into as soon as we stop and acknowledge that we are not God. When we humbly turn to the One who is at the center of this whole unfolding story.

To be with him.
To praise him.
To thank him.
To ask for help.

Manifesting and prayer have similar methods but dramatically different starting points.

The practice of manifesting is the logical outworking of self-centeredness. It's taking prayer (which God created) and practicing it without first getting off the throne.

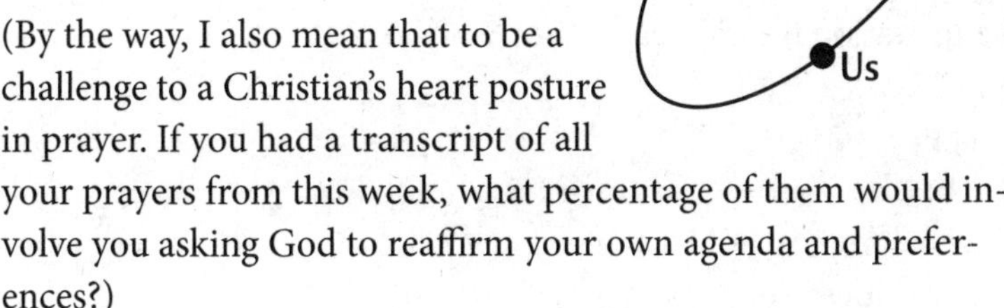

(By the way, I also mean that to be a challenge to a Christian's heart posture in prayer. If you had a transcript of all your prayers from this week, what percentage of them would involve you asking God to reaffirm your own agenda and preferences?)

Manifesting is prayer without first submitting to the hierarchy. It's prayer with self at the center. That's why manifesting (at least at a popular level) always seems to be self-centered in nature. The YouTube videos aren't titled "How to Manifest Clean Drinking Water for Kids in Need."

I bet that one wouldn't get as many clicks.

The focus is the new Jeep.
The new salary.
The new relationship.

Here are a few quotes from the beginning of *The Secret* (the 2006 hit documentary that popularized the law of attraction for a whole generation). See if you can spot the theme (it won't be hard).

"Do you know this secret gives you everything you want?"
"What kind of a house do you want to live in?"
"Do you want to be a millionaire?"
"What kind of a business do you want to have?"
"Do you want more success?"[6]

The theme is always the same: *me.*

Of course it is, since manifesting is the natural outworking of self-centered spirituality, which pushes you deeper and deeper into the me-maze.

The invitation to prayer is so much richer.

Prayer

Let's be clear: Asking for things is absolutely part of prayer. James 4:2 says, "You do not have because you do not ask God." But asking for things is only one part.

When Jesus's disciples asked him how to pray, he included this great line: "Give us each day our daily bread."

But he also invited us to pray "Father" (the reminder that we have a perfect heavenly Father). And "Hallowed be your name" (the reminder that he is at the center of the story, not us). And "Your kingdom come" (the reminder that this whole life we live is about God's kingdom, not ours). And "Forgive us our sins" (the reminder that we aren't the ones who atone for our sins). And "For we also forgive everyone who sins against us" (the reminder that God's great love for us should propel us to forgive others). And finally, "Lead us not into temptation" (the reminder that we need God's help to live the right way).[7]

Manifesting, at least at the popular level, throws out all of that, puts the self on the throne, and invites you to ask for whatever you want.

Trust me, you want God to chime in.

Typically, the things you pray about include pretty big life decisions that require a lot of wisdom. Most of the manifesting community will tell you that you know the right thing to do and you need to just trust your inner wisdom, but prayer starts from the humble place of "God, I don't know what to do here. Would you please help?"

The Creator of the universe wants to have a relationship with you—I can't stress how important that is. There's a big difference between spending time with a loving God and commanding the universe to do your bidding.

And that brings us back to me sitting in my backyard, stuck in the comparison trap.

The Power of Blessing

I hovered over the video so it played without me technically clicking.

Maybe manifesting could be my secret weapon. My spiritual steroids that propel me beyond my competition and move me up in the ranks. I thought about what that would mean for my career. And my self-esteem. And my ego.

Me. Me. Me.

The gravitational pull of the me-maze is real. And when you're caught in the comparison trap, it feels impossible to escape.

Meanwhile, the song in my headphones played on:

The Lord bless you and keep you
Make his face shine upon you and be gracious to you[8]

The song uses a blessing from the Old Testament recorded in Numbers 6:22–26:

> The LORD said to Moses, "Tell Aaron and his sons, 'This is how you are to bless the Israelites. Say to them:

"The Lord bless you
and keep you;
the Lord make his face shine on you
and be gracious to you;
the Lord turn his face toward you
and give you peace."'"

What did you notice about those words?

God didn't tell the priests, "Listen, if you give the blessing good enough, people will like how you do it more than that other guy."

No.

It's the exact opposite. The priest got the privilege of giving the blessing, not receiving it. In fact, the blessing had nothing to do with the priest. It was an invitation for the priest to help point people to the God at the center of the story.

For the last few hours, I'd been spiraling in my backyard, comparing myself with other authors, worrying that my book wouldn't be as good as theirs. Meanwhile, the lyrics to the song were screaming down into the depths of the me-maze, slowly pulling me out.

A thought popped into my mind: *What if, instead of trying to manifest book sales, I blessed other authors and their works? What if I stopped competing and started blessing?*

The words sank in. I closed my laptop, started the song over, and spent the duration of it blessing and praying for other authors.

Just a simple prayer: *May his favor be upon you.*

Every author putting out a book this year.
Every author doing their best to get the word out.

Every author I was getting jealous of.

Not out loud. No big scene. Nothing that would make my neighbors nervous. I just sat there quietly blessing everyone I could think of.

The first minute felt forced.
The second felt a bit better.
By the third minute, all the nerves were gone, the overthinking subsided, and I was just genuinely blessing others.

My me-prayers turned into we-prayers.
My mind was at peace.
My heart rate was down.

Ironically, thinking about others is the best way to feel better about yourself.

Lord, free me from me.

Praying for others is like an escape pod out of the me-maze, because it gets us out of the comparison trap. Self-centered prayers tend to be about how you can be better. Blessing others is all about God helping them be better.

When you bless others, there's a good chance God will answer the prayer and they will move up in the ranks instead of you. The flesh doesn't like that. Because if the goal is to win, that's a horrible strategy.

But maybe there's something bigger going on than those silly games we create.

Maybe spirituality is inviting us into deeper water. Where our worth is predicated not on some number but rather on being an image bearer of the Creator.

Maybe spirituality is inviting us to pray "Your kingdom come" instead of attempting to manifest "My will be done."

Maybe spirituality has the power to let the inner **Comparer**—who always feels like it doesn't measure up—off the hook.

Maybe spirituality is inviting us to think about ourselves less.

And maybe, just maybe, there's another option beyond the maze of self-centeredness.

Christ-Centered Spirituality Practice

Midday: Intercession

You began your day meditating on Psalm 23, making the conscious decision to let the Lord be your shepherd instead of being your own shepherd. You walked out your front door, ready to love and serve.

But then traffic was crazy.
Your first meeting was stressful.
Your boss critiqued you.
You got a mean text.

And on top of that, you've got this assignment due at the end of the day and you have no idea how you're going to get it done.

You were ready for a nice, calm Tuesday, but instead, it got chaotic. And without even noticing it, you ended up right back in the me-maze.

What do you do?

Sounds like a good time to stop and practice intercession.

Intercessory prayer is a fancy way of saying "praying for other people." It's one of the best Christ-centered practices you can do. Especially when you find yourself stuck in the me-maze halfway through your day.

But it's not easy.

Like we talked about in the last chapter, the flesh doesn't like it: *Don't bless others. Instead, manifest things for yourself.*

But the spirit loves it. Because besides the fact that praying for others changes things for them, it also does two things for you:

1. It helps you put God back at the center of the story.
2. As you practice putting others ahead of yourself, it helps you stop comparing yourself with them.

Intercession is like going to the gym for your soul. It may feel unnatural at first, but it's the very thing you need. And if you stick with it, you'll learn to love it.

There are a number of ways to do it, but I prefer the method I stumbled upon in my backyard when I was stuck in the comparison trap.

First, find a way to get alone. Close your door, get in your car, or go for a walk. Then turn on "The Blessing" and spend the eight minutes and twenty-seven seconds praying for other people. If you need help knowing what to pray, you can always come back to Numbers 6:24–26: "The LORD bless you and keep you; the LORD make his face shine on you and be gracious to you; the LORD turn his face toward you and give you peace."

Put simply: "Lord, bless _____ and keep them. Make your face shine upon them, be gracious to them, and give them peace."

Then move on to the next person on your list and see if you can stay in it until the song is over.

Take note of how you feel right after. For me, intercessory prayer melts away the unrelenting pressure I tend to put on myself. It has pulled me out of some of the darkest corners of the me-maze. Especially when I find myself stuck in the comparison trap.

It's simple but effective.

So, as you head into part 3, *may the Lord bless you and keep you. May the Lord make his face shine on you and be gracious to you. May the Lord turn his face toward you and give you peace. Amen.*

Layer 3 | The Avoider

From Self-Help to God's Help

Truth Statement: ***I am created in the image of a self-surrendering God.***

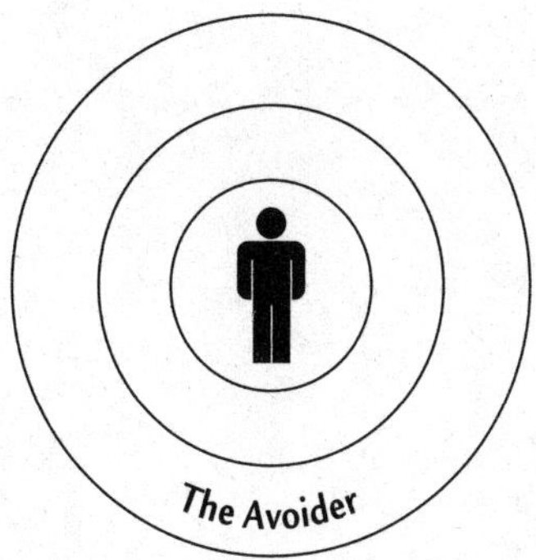

3.1: The Me-Maze (Part 3)

The Morgan Library

The subway dropped me a few blocks from my next stop—the Morgan Library & Museum.

The museum, which is home to some remarkable original manuscripts and books, began as the personal library of a wealthy banker and book collector named J. Pierpont Morgan (J. P. Morgan). I'm aware there are lots of things to do and see in Manhattan, but an afternoon perusing original manuscripts is my idea of a good time.

As I walked toward the museum, the buildings around me still felt like walls in a maze.

Even after all these years, I still get frustrated by how slowly transformation happens in my spiritual journey. I sure wish a few breakthroughs and journal entries during a day in New York would fix everything. But spirituality isn't a quick fix; it's a long, winding journey of being transformed into the image of Christ.

I looked around the busy streets of New York and thought about a hero of mine who had passed away a week earlier after a long fight with cancer. An innovative but humble man who had shown up in Manhattan thirty-four years earlier and never left. Who pastored a very unique city with grace and patience.

His name was Tim Keller.
And all his work is brilliant.

Early on in my faith journey, I was plagued by intellectual questions, and Keller's ability to use reason to explain spirituality was tremendously helpful. He was an amazing apologist and cultural commentator, but his most moving work for me is less known—it's a tiny book called *The Freedom of Self-Forgetfulness.*

Keller isn't one of those authors who drone on and on about random stories, leaving you to wonder how they all connect, before finally driving a point home (who would do that?). He gets right to the point without wasting words. So it's only forty-eight pages long. (Or if you're wired like me, fifty-four minutes on Audible.)

I threw in my AirPods, opened Audible, and hit "play." And by the time I got to the Morgan Library, I was already far enough in to be hooked.

So I bypassed the original manuscript of *A Christmas Carol,* the Gutenberg Bible, and the only surviving manuscript fragment of Milton's *Paradise Lost* and headed straight to the café (cafés in museums are just different, aren't they?). I sat and listened to the rest of the book, Americano and banana bread in front of me, scribbling notes in my journal the entire time.

Keller opens with an amazing rant on self-esteem. For centuries, he points out, it was widely believed that an inflated view of self was the main reason people did bad things.

Why would someone have an affair? What would cause them to steal or cheat on their taxes? For hundreds of years, we reasoned it was that they thought too highly of themselves. They believed they were above the law—so our job was to help them think less of themselves.

Fair enough.

But in the modern world, Keller argues, we've flipped it. We've swung the pendulum to the other side. Today the basic assumption is that people do bad things because we think too lowly of ourselves. If we just had more self-esteem, we wouldn't be drawn to that addiction or harmful behavior. So, the approach to much of therapy and spirituality has become infusing the individual with more self-confidence.

Enter positive self-talk strategies and sermons centered on the self.

So which one is it? Do we need more self-esteem or less?

Keller's basic argument in the book is that the apostle Paul took a completely different approach. He didn't try to think higher of himself, and he didn't try to think lower of himself. Instead, the gospel freed him up to simply think of himself less.

"Because the essence of gospel-humility," Keller says, "is not thinking more of myself or thinking less of myself, it is thinking of myself less."[1] He calls that space "the freedom of self-forgetfulness." And although it's hard to attain, with it comes all the rest our souls are desperate for.

Fifty-four minutes (and one extra slice of banana bread because I was on vacation) later, my journal was once again full of words blurred by tears. It wasn't just his words making me cry (I'd already heard them many times at that point); it was the depth beneath the words. A reminder that there are deeper waters that spirituality is always inviting us into. And in a world of "You Won't Believe How Fast This Works" videos like we talked about in part 2, his words were a warm blanket for my soul.

I thought about my mild panic attack in the streets of Manhattan a few hours earlier. So much of it had been brought on by shame and pain stuffed down beneath the surface, beneath the smile I painted on my face to avoid it all and convince the world I've got it all together.

A futile attempt to earn validation.

Keller's version of spirituality sounded much better.
And he got it from Paul.
Who got it from Jesus.

Gospel-humility—the freedom of self-forgetfulness.

I exhaled.

And wrote down the next role my old self still tries to play: **the Avoider.**

The Avoider

Avoiding is a less obvious attempt to keep self at the center. It tends to happen in one of two ways.

First, on those rare occasions when we actually feel like we're doing and saying all the right things, we avoid our inner brokenness by thinking too highly of ourselves.

Imagine a guy who thinks highly of himself, looking in the mirror. He's doing everything right and wants everyone to know it—*needs* everyone to know it—but deep down he's terrified of messing it all up. So he has just as much worry orbiting him.

The second (and more common for me) way we avoid is through the deflated self. For those with a deflated self, the moment we fixate on just how imperfect we are instead of participating in life, we get down on ourselves and look for ways to avoid it altogether.

Imagine a guy rocking back and forth, terrified that he'll be found out for the imperfect fraud that he is.

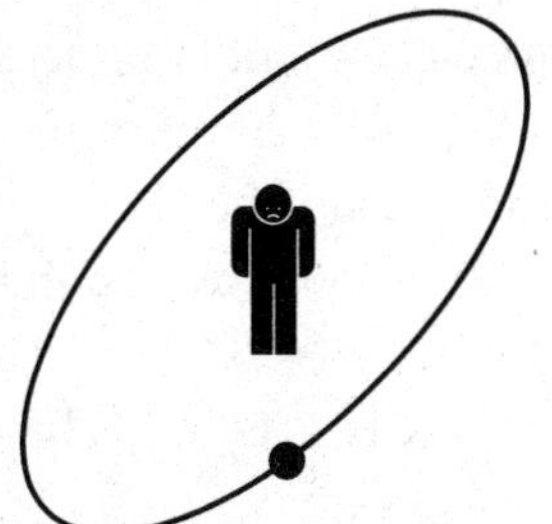

Whether you're puffed up or deflated, you're making the same mistake. You're placing yourself at the center of this story, thus inheriting the unrelenting pressure that comes with it.

When considering these depictions of the me-maze, we can see the reason we perform and the reason we compare. **The Performer** and **the Comparer** are both attempts to avoid—to cover up the blemishes, the pain, the insecurities, and the shortcomings. They're a result of the master plan of **the Avoider,** who is determined to ignore the wounded places by projecting a good self-image to the world.

On your good days, you avoid by thinking too highly of yourself.
On your bad days, you avoid by thinking too lowly of yourself.

Both throw you back into the me-maze.

The freedom of self-forgetfulness is a completely different invitation. It's an invitation to take self out of the center of the story by placing Christ back on the throne. But that's not an easy place to get to. You can't just stuff all your pain and insecurities down, slap the label of "self-forgetfulness" over them, and hope they go away.

Self-forgetfulness isn't an invitation to avoid the pain.
It's an invitation to run through it.

If you found out guests were coming over to your house for dinner, you could stuff all the clutter and junk into a back room, lock the door, and give them a tour of only the clean rooms. But if you welcomed a roommate into your house, you wouldn't be able to get away with the same strategy. Eventually, you would have to let them into the mess.

As we're about to discuss, your body is a temple of the Holy Spirit. Which means the Holy Spirit is not a dinner guest but a roommate. The Holy Spirit moves in like a roommate and begins to invite you to open those locked back rooms.

This layer is going to be uncomfortable at times.

But the pressure that is eradicated from your life when you stop trying to cover everything up is unmatchable. The freedom of knowing that God sees you—all of you—and still loves you . . . that's the freedom of self-forgetfulness.

And so, Lord, once again (one layer deeper this time), free me from me.

I sat there, nursing the last drops of my Americano, and smiled as I learned a little better how to have grace and compassion for myself and the roles the old self plays.

I love a short book as much as the next person, but I wish *The Freedom of Self-Forgetfulness* were a thousand pages. There's got to be more to this concept. Yet like the humble genius he was, Keller left it there, almost as if he were tipping his cap to the rest of us, inviting us to take the idea and run with it.

I scribbled these final lines in my journal:

I don't wanna avoid the pain anymore. I wanna experience the freedom of self-forgetfulness.

I put my pen down and threw out my trash. A tour through the museum was about to begin, so I joined them. Paying attention in part to the books in front of me and in part to the book I was writing in my mind and the sweet invitation to let go of all the pressure by thinking about ourselves less.

Of course, the method for getting to self-forgetfulness isn't self-help; it's God's help. That'll become clear in the next chapter as we discuss . . .

The old self.
The new self.
And the problem with self-help.

3.2: The Old Self, the New Self, and the Problem with Self-Help

A Simple Framework for Sanctification

Another stone whizzed through the air and found its target.

A young man named Saul stood at attention, a vicious smile on his face. This wasn't just about the stoning; it was about sending a message: *Keep talking about Jesus, and you'll be next.*

The target, a man named Stephen who couldn't stop preaching, had just fallen to his knees, and yet somehow was still talking. Saul leaned in, expecting vindictive final words:

Curses?
Pain?
Anger?

Instead, he heard something that brought unease to the deepest part of his soul: "Lord," Stephen said with his last breath, "do not hold this sin against them."[1]

"Do not hold this sin against them."

Stephen's words echoed through Saul's mind on repeat, each one adding another log to the bitter fire blazing inside.

He prays for my forgiveness? How dare he? He ought to pray for his own forgiveness.

Saul knew it was time to double down, to inflict so much harm on these followers of Jesus that the movement would come to an end. He'd taken careful note of the church. He knew which houses these followers of Jesus met in, and he intended to visit each one—dragging them off and throwing them in prison.

Jerusalem was up in arms. Saul watched as word spread of his presence, pride puffing him up with each new prisoner.

He thought of the praise he'd get from the Sanhedrin, threw back his shoulders, and set off for the next house. Praying the praise of his peers would be loud enough to drown out that awful curse Stephen had put on him: "Do not hold this sin against them."

The persecution worked.

The church scattered. Yet Saul wasn't content the way he'd thought he would be. He was sure this message would grow back like a weed unless it were stomped out completely.

So he set off for Damascus, surrounded by soldiers. He was positive that was where most of the followers of Jesus had fled, probably thinking they would be safe there. But he knew they wouldn't be. He'd arrest them and carry them back to Jerusalem to make it a public spectacle.

Saul drained the final drop from his wineskin and wiped the sweat off his brow with his forearm. The sun was directly overhead. Midday was the worst time to make this journey, but hate propelled him forward.

Suddenly, a light, exponentially brighter than the midday sun, flashed all around him. Before Saul's logical mind could process what was happening, he was on his face, shaking in fear.

"Saul, Saul," a voice boomed from every side, heavy with an authority unlike anything he'd ever heard. "Why do you persecute me?"

"Who are you, Lord?" Saul managed to ask.

"I am Jesus, whom you are persecuting."[2]

The New Self

The man in this story went on to become the apostle Paul (Saul was his Hebrew name).

The rest of his conversion story is wild. After the bright light knocked him to the ground, he went blind for three days until a man named Ananias showed up and placed his hands on him and "something like scales fell from Saul's eyes."[3]

The rest, as they say, is history. Paul stopped destroying the church and began building it. Planting churches all over the known world and later writing them letters we still read today.

When we first meet Paul, he was green-lighting murder and carrying Christians off to prison. And then he went through a dramatic conversion and spent the rest of his life building God's kingdom.

His life can be split into two very distinct acts.

Self at the center.
God at the center.

Living to build his own kingdom.
Living to build God's kingdom.

In his letters, Paul called this the old self and the new self. And that brings us back to the passage we talked about in the introduction: "Do not lie to each other, since you have taken off your old self with its practices and have put on the new self, which is being renewed in knowledge in the image of its Creator."[4]

Paul's "old self" called the shots for the first thirty-ish years of his life. When we are introduced to him, he was using spirituality for power and persecuting anyone who got in his way.

He was obviously performing.
There's no doubt he was comparing.

But the less common layer to talk about is just how much he was avoiding. Think about it: Paul needed to be right so badly that he targeted anyone who called him wrong. Nothing shouts "**Avoider**" louder than overcompensating.

His old self was convinced he was right.
His old self was convinced others were wrong.

So much so that he would tear families apart, carrying fathers and mothers off to prison just to prove how right he was.

Then he had a crazy encounter with Jesus on the road to Damascus, scales fell off his eyes, and he saw a brand-new way to live—where Jesus is the center. He devoted the rest of his life to sharing the good news of that pressure-free life.

Instead of trying to win, lose your life.
Instead of trying to be first, opt for being last.
Instead of trying to be right, love.

The good news frees you from you.

Paul talked about the old self like a costume we put on for our performance, or fig leaves we use to try to cover up who we really are. So, he instructed us to take off the old self and put on the new self.

This was a theme throughout Paul's writings:

> You were taught, with regard to your former way of life, to put off your old self, which is being corrupted by its deceitful desires; to be made new in the attitude of your minds; and to put on the new self, created to be like God in true righteousness and holiness.[5]

> We know that our old self was crucified with him so that the body ruled by sin might be done away with, that we should no longer be slaves to sin—because anyone who has died has been set free from sin.[6]

We often use the word *conversion* to explain this moment. When you decide to make Jesus the Lord of your life, the old self is gone: "If anyone is in Christ, the new creation has come: The old has gone, the new is here!"[7]

The old has gone, the new is here!

But here's where this gets complicated: What about when you experience that conversion and then, fifteen minutes later, you get really angry at someone on the highway and flip them off?

Does that mean it didn't work?
The Bible says the old has gone, but has it come back now?

How about when you raise your hand and make Jesus the Lord of your life but then years later you end up shivering on your front porch, trying to convince your roommates you are more spiritual than them?

Does that mean it didn't work?
The Bible says the old has gone, but has it come back now?

That question has plagued Christians for years. It's also one of the many reasons Paul's story is such a gift. Because although he was an absolute stud, he still wrote about the wrestling match within himself. At the end of Romans 7, he went on this epic rant summed up by this relatable verse: "I do not do the good I want to do, but the evil I do not want to do—this I keep on doing."[8]

Wait—so he took himself out of the center of the story and put Jesus at the center but still had struggles? Yes.

And that brings us to two more important words: *flesh* and *Spirit.*

Understanding these two words is the key to seeing the difference between self-help (flesh) and God's help (Spirit).

The former creates pressure.
The latter brings peace.

Flesh Versus Spirit

Paul was all too aware that, even post-salvation, he tended to try to live in his own strength. To put himself back at the center of the story and attempt to get by on his own power. He called this "living according to the flesh" rather than walking by the Spirit.[9]

"Flesh" is the Greek word *sarx,* which is a complicated word with several meanings that are important to distinguish.

When Paul compared walking in the flesh with living by the Spirit, *flesh* has a negative connotation. But that isn't true for every time you see that word in the Bible. Paul often used *sarx* to talk about the human body.[10] When this is the case, the word isn't negative; it's neutral.

Let's stop and talk about this for a second, because it's important.

It can be easy to fall into a Platonic (and Gnostic) worldview that the spirit is good but the body is bad—as though the spirit is trapped in this evil body—but that's not a biblical viewpoint.

Humans are created in the image of God. When God created creation, he called it all "very good."[11] The body isn't bad. And you've got to get that, because it's very hard to overcome struggles with self-image if you think the body is evil.

However, like we've talked about, we do have a massive problem. Sin has entered the picture. We put ourselves at the center of the story, and when we did, we started depending on our power instead of God's.

In his book *Creator Spirit,* Steven Guthrie explains it well:

> Human beings are not cursed for *having* flesh but for depending upon flesh, for depending upon what is limited, finite, and passing, rather than upon the Lord.[12]

We have a sinful nature; we are *curved in* on ourselves. And Paul also used the word *flesh* (*sarx*) to describe that tendency.

From here on out, that's how we'll be using *flesh.* So as we go, don't equate *flesh* with the body. The body isn't the problem. Putting self at the center and trying to rely on our own human autonomy is the problem.

John Coe and Kyle Strobel describe the flesh as "the weakness of human autonomy from God."[13] Walking in the flesh is trying to live without God. In a lecture on being formed by the Spirit, Coe explains that there are two ways we do this:

1. Vices of the flesh
2. Virtues of the flesh[14]

1. Vices of the Flesh

In some places, the works of the flesh are those things we're drawn to that are obviously bad: "The acts of the flesh are obvious: sexual immorality, impurity and debauchery; idolatry and witchcraft; hatred, discord, jealousy, fits of rage, selfish ambition, dissensions, factions and envy; drunkenness, orgies, and the like."[15]

In this sense, "living according to the flesh" is giving into all the worldly temptations.

But then there's another way Paul used the word.

2. Virtues of the Flesh

Paul also used *sarx* to talk about ways we ultimately try to be more like God in our own power. In Galatians 3:3, he wrote, "Are you so foolish? After beginning by means of the Spirit, are you now trying to finish by means of the flesh?"

In this context, "flesh" isn't referring to immoral practices; rather, it's referring to us doing things in our own strength. So, "living according to the flesh" can also be us trying to change ourselves in our own strength rather than "walking by the Spirit."

Enter self-help.

Self-Help

The truth about so much self-help is it ends up being a fancy way to convince us to live according to the flesh instead of walking by the Spirit—trying to achieve our goals through means of human autonomy.

I don't have a problem with a lot of the tools the self-help world preaches: Journaling, ice baths, workouts, and grounding are great supplements (I used them all this morning). They can help you wake up, get in shape, and attack your day with clarity—but they can't save you.

This narrative is peddled everywhere these days. If you just have enough confidence and self-esteem, you can help yourself right out of the me-maze.

Cut to two years later, and you end up exhausted because you've tried every new self-help book that's come out with a fresh cover, promising a new strategy to unlock the secret passage out of the me-maze. You've taken every overpriced course, and you even bought a crystal for some reason.

Only to realize you're still stuck in your own head.

Because, at some level, you were trying to save yourself.
And you can't save yourself.

Lord, free me from me.

The problem isn't self-help.
The problem is thinking self-help will save.

When you do, self-help becomes another version of "living according to the flesh." It seems to work for a while, but then it leaves you *weary* and *burdened.*[16] If you rely on the flesh to save you, you'll self-help yourself to exhaustion.

Every time you read a book, listen to a podcast, or get advice that feels "self-helpy," you're in danger of making two mistakes. The first is slapping the "dangerous" label on it and throwing out what could be good advice. The second is taking that advice and making it an ultimate thing in your life.

That's where this idea from part 1 becomes so helpful: *Who is my shepherd?*

Your goal today is to let the Lord lead as you take another step toward being transformed into the image of Christ. A workout and some sunlight will be incredibly helpful along the way. But always come back to that question and make sure you get the order right. You don't want to be your own shepherd—so don't fall into the trap of thinking you are the one helping yourself out of the pit you are in.

A little self-help can help.
But it can't save you.

And when you rely on it to save you, you may end up passed out in your own backyard.

Self-reliance, or what Paul called "living according to the flesh," puts an enormous weight on your shoulders. Because the problem with being the one in charge is you are the one in charge.

Do you know what's a lot better than self-help?

God's help.

And that takes us to one of the wildest things Jesus said. On the night he was betrayed, he told his disciples, "I tell you the truth: it is to your advantage that I go away, for if I do not go away, the Helper will not come to you. But if I go, I will send him to you."[17]

Jesus called the Holy Spirit the Helper. And he basically told the disciples, "As great as it's been to have me here in person these last few years, the Helper is the better option now."

The same is true for us today. We've got a much better option than self-help; we've got God's help. It's time to let the Helper do what the Helper does best. So, the big question for part 3: *How exactly does the Helper help?*

3.3: How the Helper Helps

From Self-Help to God's Help

There are a few elements that make a story worth hearing.

For some, it's the romance.
For some, it's the self-discovery.
For some, it's the plot twist.

Those things are all fine and great, but for me, the best part of any epic movie is when the reinforcements show up.

There's that moment when the battle looks hopeless.
The enemy is too strong.
Their schemes too evil.
The protagonist can barely stand.

And then the cavalry comes to the rescue.

Like when Gandalf shows up with the rising sun in the east, alongside Éomer and two thousand riders who charge down the hill to save Helm's Deep.

Or that moment a distant and selfish Han Solo comes out of nowhere in the *Millennium Falcon* and starts sniping TIE fighters, freeing Luke up to destroy the Death Star.

Or, of course, the crème de la crème, the climax of the Marvel Cinematic Universe, when Captain America is the only one left (barely) standing against Thanos and his army. And then you hear Sam's muffled "On your left," and an epic team of Avengers assemble.

Those moments speak to us.
They strike a deep, eternal chord in us.
Because they are a shadow of the ultimate story.

The reinforcements coming in for the rescue resonates with the new self because it reminds us of the ultimate rescue from the ultimate reinforcement.

The Helper

The story is in Acts 2. The moment Peter and the rest of the crew realized just how powerful the Helper really is.

Ministry's gotta be easier when Jesus is in the room.

I'd imagine that must've been what Peter was thinking as he watched Jesus ascend into heaven.

They had their marching orders: Make disciples to the ends of the earth.[1] No big deal. But up to that point, Jesus had been with them.

When someone needed healing—Jesus handled it.
When demons needed casting out—Jesus did it.
When food needed multiplying—Jesus took care of it.

Sure, he was training them the whole time, dropping hints like, "You give them something to eat." But their overly logical response to that statement showed how far they were from being ready to do this on their own.[2]

So Jesus's death, resurrection, and ascension put them in an interesting predicament. They were left staring up into heaven, wondering how they were going to pull this off. And to make the situation stranger, Jesus had alluded that help was on the way but he never explained exactly how it would all play out:

> I will ask the Father, and he will give you another Helper, to be with you forever.[3]
>
> The Helper, the Holy Spirit, whom the Father will send in my name, he will teach you all things and bring to your remembrance all that I have said to you.[4]
>
> I tell you the truth: it is to your advantage that I go away, for if I do not go away, the Helper will not come to you. But if I go, I will send him to you.[5]

Jesus essentially said, "Kind of a good news–bad news situation."

Bad News: I'll be leaving soon.
Good News: It's actually advantageous for you, because I'll be sending the Holy Spirit.

Imagine being Peter in that moment. *I'm sorry. Did Jesus just say it's to our advantage?*

If we were the disciples, we'd likely be tempted to put ourselves back at the center of the story at this point. *Okay, Jesus is out. We're going to need to scramble. But maybe we can still figure this out.*

We'd be thinking about our plans.
We'd be thinking about our alliances.
And we'd probably be thinking about how we could do it all while avoiding the cross.

The story picks up in the book of Acts, where we find Peter and the rest of the team left on their own, unsure what to do next. So, they did what they knew how to do: They prayed.

One day, as they were gathered together praying, there was a sound, and a mighty rushing wind filled the whole room: "They were all filled with the Holy Spirit and began to speak in other tongues as the Spirit gave them utterance."[6]

This was the moment the reinforcement came to the rescue. The promised Helper, the Holy Spirit, filled the disciples (underline that word *filled;* it's important).

The Holy Spirit isn't a "what" or an "it." The Holy Spirit is a person we are in relationship with. Said simply, the Holy Spirit is God. The third person of the Trinity, who Gordon Fee calls "God's empowering presence."[7] And that is an incredibly important distinction, because the God-centered life is an invitation into a deeply personal relationship with God.

If you know the story, you know the rest of Acts 2 is one of the most historic days in the Bible. A Jewish festival called Pentecost was at hand, meaning people were in town from all over the known world. Peter, who had recently denied Jesus three times out of fear and made a plethora of other mistakes, suddenly found his voice and preached a cuttingly brilliant message about Jesus.

Three thousand people joined the movement that day.

You'll never escape the me-maze until you understand this story.

Peter, by himself, was a mess.
Running away.
Following at a distance.
Denying he even knew his best friend, Jesus.
Weeping bitterly.
Going back to fishing.
Avoiding reality.
Caught in the me-maze and barely able to stand.

And then he heard, "On your left," and in an instant, the whole tide changed.

Peter was filled with the Holy Spirit, and it was like he completely stopped thinking and worrying about himself. Instead, he was so moved with courage and compassion that he preached a tough truth (accusing them of killing Jesus). He explained the gospel, and "they were cut to the heart."[8]

That moment changed everything. From there, the church became a picture of generous, sacrificial community. They began meeting together every day.

Learning together.
Eating together.
Selling possessions to make sure everyone was taken care of.
And God kept bringing them more and more people.[9]

Being filled by the Holy Spirit changes everything.

That last sentence is the key to the rest of this book. What does it mean to be "filled"?

We'll keep exploring that question in different ways as we go, starting with this word picture: The Holy Spirit moves in as your roommate.

Meet Your Roommate

"Hey, can you not do a workout in the living room after 10 P.M.?"

The text was from my roommate. He'd landed one of those adult jobs where he had to be at the office early. I, on the other hand, was in the middle of a sixty-day workout program called Insanity that required a lot of jumping and making noise.

I was used to a college house where we all enabled one another and nothing was off-limits. Got home at 2 A.M. and still need to work out? No worries. We all understand. In fact, we'll probably get out of bed and join you.

Then I got to the real world.

Where roommates had real jobs and decisions had real consequences. And I began realizing in real time that I knew very little about what it meant to be a good roommate.

There's a learning curve to living with roommates in the real world, because a group of people who all have their own preferences about cleanliness and quiet hours are sharing a finite space, which means preferences will be pushed. When you share space with someone, you become incredibly aware of how selfish you are.

And that is one of the thousands of reasons the presence of the Holy Spirit is such a brilliant design by God.

There are lots of ways to talk about the Holy Spirit, but one I find helpful is to think about the Holy Spirit as your roommate. The book of Acts shows the Holy Spirit moving in.

I can't tell you how many pastoral meetings I've had that have started with "I used to be able to do ____ or watch ____ or go to ____ or say ____ without thinking twice . . . but now I feel this strange conviction."

Yep . . . you've got a roommate now.

It used to be easy to avoid conviction in those areas, but not anymore. Your roommate is getting to work, forming you into the image of Christ.

Have you ever experienced this? Maybe you're feeling it as you read this book. Maybe the Holy Spirit is revealing a desire, relationship, or vice that is holding you back. For years, you've avoided thinking about it, because you didn't think you could possibly survive without it. But what if I told you the Helper is here to help you?

Here's an oversimplified explanation of Acts:

Things aren't going great.
The believers are filled with the Holy Spirit.
Things start going a lot better.

And that is an external picture of the internal journey of a believer:

We don't see how we'll ever escape the me-maze.
Then we're filled with the Holy Spirit.
And the stuff we stress about starts melting away.

Again, Steven Guthrie offers some helpful language: "The Spirit's gift is freedom from this prison of inwardness."[10]

I call it the me-maze, but "this prison of inwardness" is another great name. We get so used to thinking inwardly that it feels normal, but it's actually a prison. And the Holy Spirit moves in for the ultimate prison break. Teaching us how to surrender our own preferences, get out of our own way, and declare Jesus is Lord.[11]

Holy Spirit, free me from me.

That doesn't mean we become a nobody. Quite the opposite. Guthrie continues, "This does not mean the loss of our humanity; it means the completion of it. Humanity is made to reflect the image and glory of the God who lives in an eternal movement of self-surrender."[12] We find the fullness of our humanity by imaging a God who emptied and humbled himself.[13] And said things like, "For even the Son of Man did not come to be served, but to serve, and to give his life as a ransom for many."[14]

The Holy Spirit is in the business of re-humanizing us; he's interested not in taking our humanity but in giving it back. It's just that (and this is the rub) we were never created to be the center of the story.

And we don't always love hearing that.

Because you aren't a blank slate. You have years of pain and hardship that are whispering in your ear to make this life about you. To find convenient ways to medicate the pain in order to avoid dealing with it.

I try to cover up my pain by building a successful enough church, writing a good enough book, or hosting a powerful enough worship night. As noble as those things are at one level, they are also a feeble attempt to keep some of my rooms locked.

But my roommate has other plans. He wants to unlock those rooms with me and bring deep healing to those places.

And the same is true for you. You can do this. Whatever your locked doors are, you can find healing. But it's not easy. This is the point of the book where things start to get uncomfortable, because Spirit-led inner work isn't always fun, but it's worth it.

In the next few chapters, you are going to learn how to let the Helper guide you into the locked rooms you've spent so many years avoiding. As you do, the third layer of the me-maze will start crumbling, freeing you from you as you continue being transformed into the image of a self-surrendering God.

Chip.
Chip.
Chip.

3.4: "La, La, La"

How We Run Away from Reality

"Check the bushes behind the playground!" I shouted.

"I did," Josh reported back anxiously. "Twice. Dig up the mulch; it may be buried. I'm going to climb the fence to get a better vantage point."

He always did that.
It never worked.
He just thought it was cool.

Carmel, Indiana, was the perfect place to be a seven-year-old in the nineties. Our entire block consisted of kids our age, and all the backyards were connected. So from the moment the bell rang until somebody's parents shouted about dinner, my brother Doug and I were out there with our friends, playing football, soccer, baseball, basketball—whatever sport was in season.

On that particular evening, the timeless, reliable game of capture the flag had made its way back through the rotation.

The game is simple but brilliant.

Two teams.
Two backyards.

Each team hides their flag somewhere in their yard, and the first team to retrieve the other flag and take it back to their side wins. The catch, of course, is anytime you leave your territory and enter the other's, you're vulnerable. If you get tagged, you go to "jail" until a teammate can break you out. Which usually takes only a few minutes, but when you're seven, that is punishment enough to make you think twice before making your move.

Like I said, simple but brilliant.

The problem with capture the flag is that when both sides have an incredible hiding spot, it can turn into a bit of a stalemate. When you have to play the long game, sit back and let the other team get overzealous, put them in jail, and then attack.

Which takes every bit of self-control for a seven-year-old.

My neighbor Josh and I had succeeded—four out of six of them were in jail. We left two of our teammates standing guard and set out into enemy territory.

And then our hearts sank at the resounding call of "Dinner!"

No. Not here. Not now. We've come so far. This game can't end in a draw.

We furiously tore apart the mulch his dad had probably spent an entire Saturday placing properly.

"Josh," his mom tried again, "dinner!" This one was louder, with a hint of warning behind it. I looked over at my friend in desperation.

Josh covered his ears with his hands, shook his head, and shouted, "La, la, la."

I stared at him for a moment, my young mind trying to register what he was doing. And then we both burst into laughter and kept searching.

"*Josh,* I'm not kidding."

"La, la, la," we said in unison, covering our ears and shaking our heads, unable to stop laughing.

"I can see you," his mom said, tone moving from playful to potent.

By that point I was laughing so hard I was rolling on the ground, covered in mulch. Meanwhile, the other team had successfully freed all their teammates, located the flag, and headed back to their side.

The game was over.

I think about that moment a lot.

There was the reality Josh and I both understood: Our parents were in charge. They called the shots. Because they made all the money. And we were seven. We didn't have a shot at surviving on our own. In the end, Josh's mom was going to win. He was moments away from having to eat dinner.

That was reality.

And then our young minds stumbled upon a secret: that we had the power to ignore reality for a few minutes—*la, la, la.*

It wouldn't last long.
We knew that.

But we discovered a superpower every human possesses: the power to momentarily ignore reality.

Of course, then we all get older and realize the superpower is stronger than we ever imagined.

When you have a big decision that needs to be made, you can think through the pros and cons or you can binge-watch a show on Netflix while you doomscroll—*la, la, la.*

When deep down you know God is calling you to make a big change in your life, you can get quiet and pray about it or you can turn up your music and load your calendar—*la, la, la.*

When there's conflict with someone you love, you can step into it with grace and truth or you can sweep it under the rug and hope it goes away—*la, la, la.*

When you experience loss (whether it's a loved one, a season, or a dream), you can sit in the sacred sadness and allow yourself to grieve or you can numb the pain with whatever vice you prefer—*la, la, la.*

Or for me, when the comparison trap throws me into a spiral about the church or my writing career, I can let myself feel it and invite God into it or I can stagger around the streets of New York, trying to outrun it—*la, la, la.*

When it comes to finding convenient distractions to help us avoid what we really need to face, we are incredibly creative.

That evening in Indiana, Josh and I found out that humans are able to temporarily mute reality.
We can turn it off.
But that doesn't mean it goes away.

You can run away from reality.
But that doesn't mean reality runs away from you.

I bet you have your own version of *la, la, la.* And if you're serious about letting the Holy Spirit free you from you, you have to learn to use *la, la, la* like a tracking device. It's like a radar helping you identify the thing you're trying to avoid. We'll talk about this more in the next chapter, but when you feel yourself running to a distraction, that usually means you're close to one of those locked doors your flesh is trying to keep shut.

You can keep avoiding that place, or you can let the Holy Spirit in so he can start knocking down that wall of your me-maze.

Years later, I was walking home from dinner in Boulder, and I saw Dustin cross a really busy street with his head down and not a care in the world. It was a few days after I had brought him a brown bag to try to atone for my sins.

Two cars slammed on their brakes to keep from running him over.

One guy honked.
Another shouted.
Dustin didn't even look up.

I watched him stagger for a few moments.
His head was still down.
He was mumbling something to himself.

I couldn't take my eyes off him. A memory popped into my head: seven-year-old Josh covering his ears and saying, "La, la, la."

I started crying.

Josh and Dustin were both doing the same thing.
Dustin had just taken it to an extreme.

Josh and I had learned how to ignore reality for a few seconds.
Dustin had learned how to ignore reality for several years.

Josh's *la, la, la* was innocent mischief.
Dustin's *la, la, la* was life-alteringly serious.

Josh's frustrated his mom.
Dustin's made his entire family wonder where he was and if he was still alive. It made it impossible for him to hold down a job. And kept him stuck wandering through the deep recesses of his own me-maze.

The truth is, we all have our own *la, la, la,* and it exists somewhere on the spectrum between Josh's and Dustin's. Your method may look different from mine, but the telos is the same: Find a way to avoid the pain.

Because when you think you are the center of the universe, there's an awful lot of pressure on your shoulders, and the only way to escape for a few minutes is to try to avoid it.

The good news is, those places we try to avoid hold valuable information. When we are brave enough to face them rather than avoid them, they highlight parts of our me-maze that need to come crashing down—*if* we are brave enough to face them.

I have another note on my phone, right next to the one titled "Fig Leaves." This one is called "La, La, La." It's an ongoing list of all the ways I notice myself avoiding pain instead of facing it. Before you read any farther, I dare you to do the same. It'll help you get really good at noticing the moments you're avoiding, and that information is invaluable—it's you telling you that you're close to a locked room in your soul. When you notice yourself doing this, stop, write it down in the note, take a deep breath, and pray: *Holy Spirit, free me from me.*

I crossed the street and asked Dustin if he needed anything. He told me he was fine.

I stared into his eyes.
He stared back, trying to remember how he knew me.
But he couldn't.

Somewhere deep inside his me-maze was a human—I knew there was. But that human was lost in a complicated maze created by years of ignoring reality—*la, la, la.*

I walked home through my college town, feeling sad for Dustin. Feeling overwhelmed by how easy it is to go down a dark path.

Feeling scared for the world.
Feeling scared for myself.

When I got home, ten people were playing drinking games in my living room. I joined them—*la, la, la.*

3.5: Holy, Holy, Holy

How to Run into Reality

"Before the summer, I was seeing the world in black and white, and now I see it in color."

I'd dropped that line four times, but it was true. I was driving from my parents' house in Phoenix to my college house in Boulder after another transformative summer leading mission trips in Costa Rica.

That meant thirteen hours in a car by myself, so I was calling my friends to hear about their summers. When they'd ask me about mine, I'd gush into stories about wild adventures and answered prayers, all of which culminated in that line about seeing the world more brightly.

At the time, I didn't know why.
Looking back, I do.

For three months, I was living in reality. I didn't have access to any of the vices I usually used to avoid reality.

No phone.
No computer.
Once a week, I'd jump on a friend's laptop to tell my parents I was alive, and that was it.

For three months, I was free from me.
I didn't think about myself.
I served others.
Loved others.

It felt phenomenal—like I was finally free from the unrelenting pressure of self-centeredness.

I hung up the phone with my friend Chris and got ready to call Brandon. But before I did, I noticed my check-engine light was on and it killed my high. My stomach sank. I still had six hours left on my road trip.

Brandon and I caught up and talked about the upcoming semester. The whole time, the check-engine light mocked me.

An hour later, I stopped to fill up my tank and bought a roll of duct tape. When I got back into my car, I tore off a piece and covered the check-engine light.

Problem solved—*la, la, la.*

The Check-Engine Light
Reality can be uncomfortable.

Taking your car into a shop and letting some mechanic, who you're pretty sure is going to rip you off, look at it while you sit on a cold, hard chair and drink crappy coffee isn't comfortable. It's a lot easier to put a piece of tape over the check-engine light and get on with living your life.

But the light isn't the actual problem; it's an indicator that something is going on beneath the hood. Putting a piece of tape over the indicator isn't fixing anything.

And what's true about cars is also true about the human soul.

God built us with indicators. But listening to those indicators isn't always easy and is hardly ever convenient. It's a lot easier to put a piece of duct tape over the check-engine light and keep going.

And we've created cover-ups that are much more sophisticated than duct tape:

Say you had a really tough meeting with your boss and you're terrified you're going to lose your job. You should give yourself a chance to feel that fear by sitting with it or talking to someone about it, but instead, you buy a massive meal on your drive home and spend your night scrolling on your phone looking for reasons to be outraged about other people's lives instead of facing your own—*la, la, la.*

Or say you have a massive decision to make and three small decisions. And now the small ones feel like massive ones, so you avoid anyone who needs any answers from you all week and instead work on something that doesn't really matter—*la, la, la.*

Or maybe that's still too mild for you and you resonate more with Dustin's side of the spectrum. Where you're constantly looking for ways to not be in your right mind.

Every day is different.
Every situation is different.
Every story is different.

But the truth remains: You can't run away from reality forever.

You can put a piece of tape over the check-engine light on your dashboard, but that doesn't fix anything. If you want God to free you from you, you're going to have to take the power back from your inner **Avoider.**

So, what do we do? How do we invite the Holy Spirit to start chipping away at this third layer of the me-maze? To answer that question, let's wind the clock back to the eighth century B.C. and talk about a wild day the prophet Isaiah had in Jerusalem.

The Throne Room

Jerusalem had seen better days—King Uzziah had just passed away, and Israel was in grave danger. Isaiah knew there was hope for the future. But first, judgment for all the rebellion and idolatry.

His message would mostly fall on deaf ears, at least in the short term—he knew that. But he also knew that part wasn't up to him. His job was to speak the words God gave him with courage.

Isaiah closed his eyes and was immediately brought into a vision. He was in the temple, and God was in the middle, seated on a throne, high and exalted. The throne was surrounded by seraphim (angels with six wings), each crying out, "Holy, holy, holy is the LORD Almighty; the whole earth is full of his glory."[1]

Without the luxury of being able to **bold** or *italicize* words, ancient writers often used repetition to add emphasis. Repeating a word was like saying "very." In this passage (and in Revelation 4, where John had a similar experience), the angels tripled down on the word *holy.*

Not just holy . . .
Not just holy, holy . . .
The Lord is holy, holy, holy!

Isaiah was deeply moved by the entire situation. And in the presence of God's perfection, he immediately felt what every one of us would feel: the weight of his own imperfection.

> "Woe to me!" I cried. "I am ruined! For I am a man of unclean lips, and I live among a people of unclean lips, and my eyes have seen the King, the LORD Almighty."[2]

Notice Isaiah wasn't able to avoid anything in God's presence. He wasn't able to compartmentalize his less glamorous qualities; he just spewed it all out: "I am a man of unclean lips."

You know that moment when you used to make a joke around your friends and never thought twice about it—but then you make the same joke while your less-deranged friend is present and you suddenly feel weird about it?

Same joke.
Different audience.

That's what I picture Isaiah feeling, except multiplied by a million. Isaiah was a stud, a major prophet.[3] But in the presence of a holy God, all he could say was, "I am ruined."

Then in a beautiful portrayal of the gospel, seven hundred years before Jesus, Isaiah said:

> One of the seraphim flew to me with a live coal in his hand, which he had taken with tongs from the altar. With it he touched my mouth and said, "See, this has touched your lips; your guilt is taken away and your sin atoned for."[4]

Atonement (a meaning you now know) seven hundred years before the cross. Because God's plan for his people has never been fig leaves and shame. . . . It's always been redemption and relationship.

Isaiah saw a vision.
But actually, he got a glimpse of reality.

The eternal reality that is happening right now in the throne room and will be all of our experience when Jesus returns. And in that reality, the only words that seem necessary are "Holy, holy, holy."

Run Into Reality

When self is at the center of the story, reality is the enemy. You are the one in charge. It's up to you to perform. And anyone, anything, or any situation that may expose you as a fraud becomes a threat.

So you do everything you can to avoid reality—*la, la, la.*

But if we could just see what Isaiah saw. If we could just understand that we are not sitting on the throne but that God is. The God who created us in his image. The God who went to great lengths to atone for our sins. The God who is Lord over all of this. If we could just see that truth, our response would always be "Holy, holy, holy."

That is the key to running into reality instead of away from it.

Take conflict, for example. The flesh feels threatened by conflict. After all, the old self thinks it's in charge, so if someone has a critique for you, they're a threat to your kingdom. Your flesh senses conflict and says, "La, la, la."

For some, it's fight.
For others, it's flight.
For all of us, it's *la, la, la.*

But the invitation of Christ-centered spirituality is to stop playing that game. After all, you're part of "a kingdom that cannot be shaken."[5] So you can enter conflict with grace and truth.

Self-centered spirituality preaches "La, la, la."
Christ-centered spirituality preaches "Holy, holy, holy."

The old self is motivated by fear.
The new self is motivated by love.

When you remember God's got this, every moment (even the uncomfortable ones) becomes holy. The new self knows God is always with you, so it runs into reality—*holy, holy, holy.*

One of the best ways to practice letting the Holy Spirit into the locked back rooms in your house is to trade in *la, la, la* for *holy, holy, holy.*

I literally say it out loud.

When book sales are making me spiral and everything in me wants to turn to a vice to medicate and avoid—*la, la, la*—I'll stop, acknowledge that the Holy Spirit is in this process with me, and then say out loud, "Holy, holy, holy."

Try it.

Trade in *la, la, la.*
For *holy, holy, holy.*

When someone sends you a DM critiquing you for something and everything in you wants to shoot back a snarky rebuttal, what if instead you reminded yourself that you aren't a house of cards? You aren't worried about your self-image nearly as much as reflecting God's image, so this critique is an opportunity for honest reflection—*holy, holy, holy.*

When that dark memory from your past pops up and everything in you wants to stuff it back down, take a deep breath instead and remember that the Holy Spirit will hold your hand and lead you back into that memory to let you grieve it, get angry, be embarrassed, or feel whatever else you need to from it so you can let it go—*holy, holy, holy.*

When there is drama in your family and you just want to exit stage right and avoid the whole situation, remember instead that Paul invited us to be "patient in conflict"[6] and see it as an opportunity to come closer together—*holy, holy, holy.*

We can run away from reality—*la, la, la.*
Or we can run into reality—*holy, holy, holy.*

Try it out. But be warned: When you start doing this exercise, you'll begin to notice just how much your inner **Avoider** runs from. Take it slow and have grace for yourself.

The inner work isn't easy.
It's easier to avoid it all.
Most people do.

But letting the Spirit into the locked rooms you try to avoid is the way to bring those walls of your me-maze down.

Holy Spirit, free me from me.

It was 9 P.M. by the time I pulled into Boulder—tired but excited to be home. I turned onto Broadway to head to my house on Sixteenth Street.

Dustin was at the intersection.
My welcome committee back to Boulder.

Except he wasn't very welcoming. His beard and hair hadn't been cut or combed since I'd last seen him in May. He was sitting on the median and rocking back and forth while yelling at himself.

I tried to say hi.
It didn't go well.

Whatever high he'd experienced that evening was wearing off.
And he was being forced to face reality without it.

Dallas Willard once said that reality is "what you run into when you are wrong."[7] Dustin had run away from reality for a few hours, but now he was being forced to confront it head-on.

Of course, that made me feel terrible for him. And then I glanced down at the duct tape on my own dashboard and realized I was doing the same thing.

I thought about the last three months when I'd had no way to run away from reality, so I'd run right into it.
When I started feeling nervous before a new team would arrive, I'd tell someone and we'd talk about it.
When I was feeling stressed out by all the traffic and the loud kids who were now getting under my skin, I couldn't pull out my phone and scroll, so I'd talk to God about it.
When I was feeling overwhelmed, I'd sneak away with my journal and write about it.

But then I got back to the real world and started running. The light turned green, and I drove off to my college home. As I drove, a line ran through my mind:

Either you run into reality . . .
Or reality runs into you.

That was true about Dustin.
It was also true about me.
And it's true about you.
We all have a level of *la, la, la.*

Two months later, my car overheated in the middle of the highway.

3.6: A Breath Prayer for the Avoider

Stop and Pray

If you're wired like me, part of you is screaming at this book to move on from all this "stop avoiding your inner pain" talk.

Don't worry—we're about to.

But for the next two minutes, let's run straight into it. As you read the last two chapters, did you have a *la, la, la*? Was there a thought, feeling, memory, or decision that you kept trying to avoid?

Don't judge it. Don't overthink it. Just practice letting the Holy Spirit (your roommate who is leading you on the journey of being transformed into the image of Christ) into that locked room.

Bring your *la, la, la* to the forefront of your mind and invite the Holy Spirt into it as you read 1 Corinthians 6:19: "Do you not know that your bodies are temples of the Holy Spirit?"

Inhale: I am a temple of the Holy Spirit.
Exhale: Holy Spirit, free me from me.

Inhale for five seconds.
Exhale for five seconds.
Do this ten times.

3.7: Neither Puffed Up nor Deflated

Why the Rest You Seek Depends on Being Filled with the Holy Spirit

"One step back!"

Roger's dad was sporting a full-on referee outfit for his son's birthday—whistle and all. We'd been locked in intense competitions all day, and everything had now come down to the egg toss.

If you didn't go to birthday parties in the nineties, let me catch you up. The rules of an egg toss are simple:

Toss the egg to your partner.
If it doesn't break, you advance to the next round.
Take a giant step back and repeat.

At Roger's birthday party, everyone made it through the first few rounds. But then eggs started breaking. Because kids either dropped them or put too much velocity into the throw.

The key to the egg toss is finesse.

I was teamed up with Tim.
We were locked in.

"Step back!" Roger's dad said again.

The crowd was on Roger's side, which made sense. It was his party. But you better believe my competitive seven-year-old self couldn't have cared less that it was his birthday. I was going to win the competition; he could cry if he wanted to.

I dropped my hands as the egg hit them and managed to catch it safely. Roger did the same. I had to hand it to him; the kid was good at egg toss.

"Step back."

My team and Roger's team were the only two remaining. We had been for a while, but the next step was no joke.

I threw up the Hail Mary.
Then I watched and prayed.
The egg broke open as soon as it hit Tim's hands. It sprayed all over his shirt. My heart sank.

Roger's toss was several feet short, but his teammate lunged forward to catch it. As the egg fell down, my hope went up. But then the impossible happened . . .

The egg hit the ground without breaking.
The crowd erupted.
Roger won.

(At this point, you probably think this is going to turn into a redemptive story of getting out of the me-maze and learning to celebrate someone on their birthday, but you would be mistaken.)

I was livid.

"Soft hands, Tim," I shouted, stomping toward him and demonstrating how he should have dropped his hands. "We talked about this."

The crowd looked down on me, shunning me like the loser I was.

Roger's dad handed him the trophy.
Everyone cheered.

I fought back tears.

When you're a competitive seven-year-old, winning and losing come with a steep learning curve.

Winning is euphoric.
Losing is demoralizing.

Winning makes you feel like everything will work out.
Losing makes you feel like nothing will be okay ever again.

Winning makes you feel like royalty.
Losing makes you feel like a peasant.

And in second grade, winning was a drug that I couldn't get enough of. So my life oscillated between the high of winning and the low of losing. My ego was always either puffed up in the luster of victory. Or deflated in the misery of defeat.

Puffed up.
Or deflated.

And it's one thing for a seven-year-old to feel that way in the heat of competition, but it's another thing for a thirty-something-year-old to feel that way while obsessively checking Amazon to see where his book ranks against other writers'.

Puffed up when I was climbing in the ranks.
Deflated when I was falling.

If you think about it, the old self really has only two outcomes. When you believe you are the center of the story and the rest of the world revolves around you, you feel the spotlight shining brightly on you, and you know that it's time to entertain and impress—and that it's going to go either really well or really poorly.

They'll either cheer.
Or boo.

And you'll leave the room feeling validated.
Or miserable.

And then the next room you walk into, the process will happen all over again.

Puffed up.
Or deflated.

Even if it all goes well, the best the old self can hope for is being overinflated.

Puffed Up

Have you ever overinflated a balloon? If so, you know how delicate it is. One little bump and it will pop.

An overinflated ego works the same way. It presents itself as secure, grand, and important, but it's actually fragile.

That's why some of the most talented people in the world are also the most insecure. As the old saying goes, *Never meet your heroes.*

Think about the last time you talked to someone with a puffed-up ego. It probably felt like the conversation was one wrong word away from blowing up, so you tiptoed around, choosing each word carefully.

Or maybe you've been the one who is always on the edge of having your confidence shattered. You might build up a fortress and do your best to protect yourself—digging a moat around your own little private castle, drenching yourself with positive self-talk, and surrounding yourself with an entourage to stand guard and shield you from the outside world—but you can't avoid critiques or failures forever. Sooner or later, the world is going to break through.

Self-confidence and positive self-talk are great things. But here's a fair question: If everyone is so "confident," then how come everyone is so easily offended? Could it be that what we call confidence is actually a puffed-up ego?

The solution isn't to puff up even more.
The solution is to get out of the center of the story.

Deflated

Life is full of ups and downs. When self is at the center and the world does break through, it takes all the wind out of your sails. Anchoring our worth to the world leads to disaster. When we try to validate ourselves, we ultimately end up feeling puffed up on our good days or embarrassed on our bad. Because when it's on you to build your kingdom and it comes crashing down, you're going to feel defeat, exhaustion, and despair.

But Jesus didn't play that game.
He didn't care about status.

He didn't need praise, because his ego wasn't deflated.
And insults didn't get to him, because he wasn't puffed up.

When he rode into Jerusalem on Sunday and the crowd cheered, shouting "Save us!"[1] it didn't inflate his ego. And on Friday, when the same crowd shouted "Crucify him!"[2] it didn't leave him deflated.

Remember, Jesus is the model we are shooting for. He is the example. And here's the next massive piece to the puzzle:

He was full of the Holy Spirit.[3]

That's why you never see Jesus playing that game. In fact, when his disciples began arguing over who was the greatest, he grabbed a towel and a basin of water, got down on the ground, and began washing feet.[4]

That invitation to be filled with the Holy Spirit is now available to all of us. And it's an essential part of this journey of finding freedom from ourselves, because in a world that preaches self-help, Scripture offers God's help.

The Helper, the Holy Spirit, is here.

The old self will always be left asking if it's enough. And every moment of every day, we have three options for responding:

Option 1: We can work to prove our own worth (puffed up).
Option 2: We can give up and admit defeat (deflated).
Option 3: We can let the Spirit answer that question for us (filled).

Filled

Option 3 is the cheat code to life: "Be filled with the Spirit."[5]

Paul prayed an epic prayer for his friends in Ephesus: "I pray that you, being rooted and established in love, may have power, together with all the Lord's holy people, to grasp how wide and long and high and deep is the love of Christ, and to know this love that surpasses knowledge—that you may *be filled* to the measure of all the *fullness* of God."[6]

"Be filled" comes from the Greek verb *pléroó,* which means "to make complete."[7] Study any stream of spirituality long enough, and you'll eventually realize that completeness is what all of them are getting after. We all know something is wrong, and we all believe that if we can just do enough stuff, we can feel fulfilled (or enlightened or whatever other word we use to get at the same idea).

The problem is, the fruit of all that effort is the unrelenting pressure of doing spirituality in your own strength. After all, you'll have a few good days here and there, but then you'll be responsible for filling the tank all over again. Self-centered spirituality is like trying to keep a bucket full of holes filled with water.

Paul was saying something wildly different. He knew all the fulfillment we look for is found only in God. So, he prayed that we'd have an increased capacity to appreciate just how loving this God who is at the center of all of this is, because the Holy Spirit is the one who does the filling.

Filled is very different from *inflated.*

And that takes us back to Roger's party.

It was later revealed that Roger was cheating. His dad hadn't given him a regular egg like the rest of us. His egg was hard boiled—oldest trick in the book.

It's a cheat code to winning the egg toss.

A standard uncooked egg is like a puffed-up ego. It's fragile, which is the whole point of the game. It doesn't matter how safely your teammate tries to catch it; there's a good chance it's going to explode.

And if you have a hollowed-out egg, it's like having a deflated ego. Even if you throw it as hard as you can, there's no chance it's making it across the field. It's too light. The wind will take it.

However, there is a third option. The hard-boiled egg has enough weight to fly *and* enough density to sustain impact.

It's not deflated; it's full.
It's not fragile; it's full.

It's *hard* to *boil* a truth down into an analogy without getting it *scrambled*, but this one gets close. The hard-boiled egg is like being filled with the Spirit. It's not just the cheat code to winning the egg toss; it's the cheat code to life.

When you are filled with the Spirit, you aren't arrogant.
You aren't anxious or avoidant.
You aren't blown by the wind or tiptoeing on eggshells.

You are safe.
You are secure.
You are filled with the Spirit.

Every inhale is a reminder that you aren't deflated.
Every exhale is a reminder to not be puffed up.

That's what I've been getting at through all these breath prayers.

Inhale: I am not dust.
Exhale: I am not divine.

Inhale: The Lord is my shepherd.
Exhale: I lack nothing.

Inhale: I am a temple of the Holy Spirit.
Exhale: Holy Spirit, free me from me.

Realizing you aren't the center of the story takes the pressure off you. And when you are filled with the Holy Spirit, you can stop running away from conflict and become "patient in trouble."[8] Because you know that God will work through the conflict—*holy, holy, holy.*

When you are filled with the Holy Spirit, you can begin to "get rid of all bitterness."[9] Because even though people will make awful mistakes in this fallen world, you can believe that God is working right in the middle of it—*holy, holy, holy.*

When you are filled with the Holy Spirit, you can stop avoiding your own shortcomings and start boasting about your weaknesses.[10] Because in your weakness, God makes you strong—*holy, holy, holy.*

The pressure of self-centeredness may be unrelenting, but the freedom of a Christ-centered life is never ending!

To truly experience that freedom, you have to be willing to let God bring down the final layer of the me-maze—**the Controller.** So, one last Christ-centered spirituality practice, and then on to the final layer of this book.

Christ-Centered Spirituality Practice

Evening: Meditation

Enjoying a cup of tea just before bed is one of my favorite parts of the day.

When all the day's to-do lists are completed, all the doors are locked, and I'm retiring for the night, it's time for tea. My way of telling my body that we're done and it's time to check out.

But imagine if I asked you if you wanted some tea and then I dipped the tea bag in the hot water for only one second before tossing the bag in the trash.

"Thanks for the hot water," I imagine you'd say. "But I'm good."

That's not how you make tea.
Tea has to steep.

And that's how I think about our final Christ-centered spirituality practice—my go-to nighttime routine: meditation.

Meditating on Scripture is the act of letting a Bible passage steep in your soul like a bag of tea in your mug. It's one thing to read, "Come to me, all you who are weary and burdened, and I will give you rest,"[1] in your Bible-in-a-year plan. Reading and studying Scripture is a great practice, but meditation is something different. It's an invitation to slow down and sit with it. To read it over and over again, the way we have in this book, and let Scripture begin to sink into your heart and become part of who you are.

To let it steep.

By the way, *meditate* is a word we get from Scripture. The very first psalm begins, "Blessed is the one . . . whose delight is in the law of the Lord, and who *meditates* on his law day and night."[2] The Hebrew word the psalmist used here is *hagah.* It means "to ponder or to murmur."[3] The psalmist invites us to ponder and murmur Scripture. That's a very different practice from how a lot of streams of spirituality talk about meditation today.

One common way modern self-help practices use meditation is transcendental meditation (TM). The basic idea of TM is to take a mantra (a word or phrase that is, in this practice, typically meaningless; it's just a sound that is used to quiet your thoughts and help you go deeper) and say it over and over again as you sink into your own mind. The classic example is to think of your mind as an ocean. Although there may be wild waves on the surface, deep down beneath all that, the ocean is silent and calm.

To be fair, that's a pretty good illustration of my mind. And learning to sink beneath the surface can be really helpful. Lots of research has been done to show health benefits of these types of strategies. They can calm your nervous system, reduce stress, and all that.

The problem (by now you know where I'm heading) is that this technique and many others like it put self at the center. The goal is to plunge into the depths of your mind to find your truth as if you were your own shepherd. When the focus is self, you may experience a temporary sense of calm, but if you are your own guide, then practices like these also move you deeper into the me-maze at the same time.

I've had so many pastoral meetings that have begun with, "I've been practicing TM for the last six months, and it was great at first, but now I feel off. And I can't figure out what's wrong. And I am trying to get back to feeling good."

Notice the pattern—me, me, me.
The pressure of self-centeredness is never ending.

Plus, when self is at the center, you become your own tour guide through terrain you've never been to. Which is why there are so many stories of TM going to dark places.

The phenomenal news is that you don't have to be your own guide. You can let the Lord be your shepherd. Scripture invites us to meditate on God's words. To put God at the center by reflecting deeply on a passage in the Bible.

As I said above, meditating is my go-to nighttime practice. I have friends who hit their stride at the end of the day. Who do their best work late into the night. I'm not one of them. There's a point when my mind says, "No more." So any spirituality practice that involves thinking too much is out. For me, the night isn't a time to think. It's a time to meditate. It's a time to be grateful for everything the day brought (the good, the bad, and the ugly). It's a time to acknowledge my own limitations as a finite human and let God be God.

Before you head into part 4 of this book, take three minutes and try biblical meditation. You can even set a timer on your phone for three minutes if you need a shot clock. Use the three minutes to meditate on Matthew 11:28–30 by following these four steps:

Step 1: Read the passage all the way through.
Step 2: Read it again and notice what line or phrase stands out to you.
Step 3: Ask God if there is anything he wants to speak to you about that line or phrase.
Step 4: Read it again and then sit quietly with it for as long as you are able.

> Come to me, all you who are weary and burdened, and I will give you rest. Take my yoke upon you and learn from me, for I am gentle and humble in heart, and you will find rest for your souls. For my yoke is easy and my burden is light.

As you unplug for the night, let the Word of God steep in your soul and become part of who you are. Don't be afraid to let God into the locked rooms of your soul. The places where you tend to keep him out. God already knows everything you try to hide, and he still loves you.

So let him into the pain, the shame, and the insecurity. And watch as the third layer of your me-maze comes crashing down and you begin experiencing some rest for your soul.

Layer 4 | The Controller

From Self-Care to Soul Care

Truth Statement: ***I am created in the image of a self-giving God.***

4.1: The Me-Maze (Part 4)

Central Park

The sun reflected off Conservatory Water—the model boat pond on the east edge of Central Park. The perfectly still water felt like a reflection of my soul for the first time in months.

Beej and I were sitting on a bench and staring at the pond after a long walk through the park where I'd caught him up on everything I'd just experienced. On the new thought (which is actually really old) about how God is obviously the center of all of this and how grasping that is the key to everything, because it allows us to trade in an obsession with self-image for an invitation to embrace being made in God's image.

My friend Beej is a gift to the world. We were roommates for years, and despite being polar opposite people, we've always understood each other.

I'm an introvert.
He's an extrovert.

I overthink everything.
He reminds me to chill out and enjoy life.

That was his conclusion once again as I explained St. Patrick's Cathedral and my existential crisis on the streets of Manhattan.

He listened.
He gave me space.
And then he told me I think too much.

We laughed. And the sun reflected off the pond.

A man sat on a nearby bench, playing the trumpet. His long gray hair was combed back neatly. He was wearing all white, except for an old worn and torn yellow sports coat. A coat that had probably been obnoxious in its glory days before it was humbled by years of life. He was slouching comfortably on the bench and playing "La Vie en Rose." A song about seeing the world through rose-colored glasses.

To me, it's the song from *Wall-E*. That depressing Pixar movie about the robot living in a post-apocalyptic future where humans have become the center of their own worlds. Reclining in their hover chairs, staring at screens, getting anything they want delivered to them—fit-less, lifeless, and bored.[1] A brilliant depiction of the extreme outworking of the me-maze.

The song was soothing. It had us in a trance. For a moment, everything was calm.

I wasn't spiraling.
I wasn't overthinking.
I wasn't thinking about myself at all.

I was free from me.

One of the song's notes went flat as a lady in a red dress walked by.

"Betty," the musician said, smoothly lowering the trumpet and setting it in his lap.

The woman, who was walking her dog, stopped, turned, and smiled. She inched closer to the man, and they exchanged pleasantries. Her small black puppy tugged at the leash, annoyed by the stop.

She sat.
The music stopped.
Apparently, the show was over.

I come from a world where we don't miss opportunities to create moments. People come to church to feel something. To be set free. To get answers to their most pressing questions. It's my job to facilitate those moments. To create space in a world full of self-centered noise and distraction. To remind people there is better news. That God is on the throne and that he cares about them deeply.

I love creating that space for people. I'm all for it. But then sometimes it leaves me hyperventilating in the streets of New York. It's a double-edged sword. On one hand, it's an honor. In a world inundated with messages about the self, I have the opportunity to remind people of what is always true: that God is at the center of all of this, not us.

On the other hand, it can so quickly turn into something I try to control.

I'd imagine you have your own version of that predicament. You fall in love, and it's amazing, but eventually a fear of losing that love or not being enough for that person leads you to start trying to control the relationship. You land your dream job and are ecstatic for a day but then immediately feel unqualified and try to control people's perception of you. The me-maze is always beckoning us to return to the center of our story.

The never-ending performance.
The comparison trap that comes with it.
All the ways we try to avoid the bad.

At the bottom of all of that is control—the flesh's last-ditch effort to hold on to the throne.

Beej and I stared at the pond and pretended we weren't eavesdropping.

Betty was officially back in town for the summer. It was decidedly "warm enough for her taste." He assured her he was glad she was back. Her presence was "like a new sunrise after a long Manhattan winter." Trumpet-guy, it turned out, was real smooth.

Beej and I began scheming how to buy an apartment right next to Central Park. I pulled up Zillow. We looked at the prices and laughed. Then decided that one day one of us would probably hit the Powerball.

I pulled out my journal.

We have nowhere to be. Nothing to do. We're seeing *The Lion King* on Broadway tonight, but that's it. In this moment, as we stare at this pond, I can feel new life waking up in me. Life beyond the me-maze. As if my attempts at control are melting away, like a spring day after a long Manhattan winter.

I decided trumpet-guy's line was better than mine, gave up on writing, and started budgeting for weekly Powerball tickets.

Betty finally gave in to her puppy's demand to keep moving. She and trumpet-guy hugged. She stood and continued her afternoon stroll. Trumpet-guy began a new song, not the least bit worried that he hadn't finished the last.

I stared at the pond.
The pond stared back.

It was an afternoon when nothing happened. And I haven't been able to stop thinking about it since.

Do you have memories of days like that? Of moments when both your inner and your outer worlds seemed to be at peace? Yet how often do we miss those because we're so wrapped up in trying to cling to the illusion that we're in charge or that we're at the center?

It's haunting how quickly we sprint back into the me-maze. Think about what's at the bottom of so many of the games we play. Performing, comparing, avoiding—they're all feeble attempts at control.

The Controller is that final layer that is so hard to break through. This challenge has existed ever since Adam and Eve ran, hid, blamed, and sewed together fig leaves in the garden.

But remember, your new self "is being renewed in knowledge in the image of its Creator" (Colossians 3:10). The Holy Spirit is slowly but surely chipping away at all those walls of your me-maze.

Chip.
Chip.
Chip.

You are being transformed into the image of Christ. This process of renewal is lifelong, but little glimpses—like the one I got to experience in Central Park—are worth celebrating. In spirituality, they are often right on the other side of letting go of control.

So to finish our journey together, let's get really practical and talk about how to get there by discussing . . .

Control and revival.
Control and relationships.
And how psychedelics and astrology are weak efforts to control eternal truth.

4.2: Revival

An Invitation to Let Go of Control

The stars are always brighter when you drive up into the Rocky Mountains. But one night during the first week of my final year in college, I didn't make the drive joyfully. I was frustrated.

Instead of going back to Costa Rica that summer, I'd decided to intern at a ministry called the Annex, a college ministry that had been playing a pivotal role in my faith journey.

In the summer, the ministry was a lot more laid back since most of the students were gone. So my focus had been asking God to move in a powerful way in the fall. We wanted the first service of the new school year to be the beginning of a move of God. We wanted God to shake the auditorium and fill us with his Spirit like he had for the disciples in Acts. We wanted revival to break out on our campus.

Revival is a word we use to describe moments in history when the work of God seems to accelerate exponentially. There have been multiple monumental moments over the last two millennia—and as the new school year drew near, we spent the summer praying it would happen again.

We gathered a group of people to pray every Wednesday on Farrand Field (a field right in the middle of campus that most students use to either throw a Frisbee, smoke, or throw a Frisbee while they smoke). Every week, we prayed that the first Annex of the new school year would be different.

Then the fall finally came and, with it, the first service we'd spent so much time praying for. Students showed up. We sang. We heard a message. And people laughed and hugged as they caught up with friends in the lobby.

I didn't stick around for all of that.
I left, furious and frustrated.

I wanted more.
More people.
More tears.
More salvations.
More goosebumps.

I wanted it so badly that I drove up a mountain to voice my annoyances to God. I reminded him of all those Wednesdays we'd sacrificed out in that field praying. I reminded him of the numbers I'd asked for, a quota we hadn't hit.

I was exhausted.
I was angry.

And Jesus's offer, "Come to me, all you who are weary and burdened, and I will give you rest,"[1] sounded too good to be true.

Because I thought I'd done that, but apparently it hadn't worked. Instead of getting rest, I just got a heavier burden that made me even *more* weary.

Fifteen years later, that memory still makes me cringe. I have enough perspective to see how much of a control issue I had (and probably still have) in spiritual moments like those. That night and that first service should have been all about God, but I found a way to make it about me.

At one level, my cry for revival was pure.
But then there was an uglier layer beneath it.

I was looking for an emotive experience.
I was hoping for tears.

I didn't just want the night to ignite a revival in our city; I wanted reporters to write articles and historians to write books about how it was all sparked because a few college kids had the faith to pray every Wednesday for a whole summer. In other words, I wanted it to be about me. And I wanted it to be done on my timetable. All the prayers were simply my way of trying to control the outcome.

The better prayer that night in the mountains would've been, *Lord, free me from me.*

Did you know the pressure of self-centeredness is never ending?

If you resonate with any of this and if Jesus's invitation, "Come to me, all you who are weary and burdened, and I will give you rest," sounds like an empty promise to you, there's a good chance control is the thing standing in the way. It could be that the frustration and disappointment are highlighting a way you are still trying to tell God what to do, instead of the other way around.

You likely have your own version of how you try to control your spiritual journey.

Maybe you (like me) tend to turn God into a vending machine. Where you decide you'll put in a certain number of songs worshipping or hours praying and, in return, God will move in the exact way you want him to.

Maybe you figured at this point you wouldn't have any questions left about faith or struggle with any doubts, but you still do. So you try to control those thoughts by pushing them into a back room in your soul and locking the door—*la, la, la.*

Maybe you've become impatient with the long work of God and have started scouring the internet for those quick-fix solutions. You still show up to church and read your Bible and all that, but if you're honest, you're way more interested in practices where you can be at the center.

The list goes on and on.

If I could speak to my younger self, I'd remind him that the soul rest that Jesus talked about is possible but that Jesus began that famous teaching with three essential words: "Come to me." This radical invitation calls us to stop trying to control outcomes and focus more on surrender and trust. Because as image bearers, we get to play a pivotal part in this unfolding narrative God is telling. So much of which is above our pay grade.

The truth is, that service at the Annex was incredible. I've had conversations with two friends I respect deeply who say that night was a massive turning point for them. Which means, when I was up in the mountains shouting at God for not moving, they were telling their friends all about how God *was* moving. That's about as humbling a realization as you can get.

I couldn't see it.
Because I was trying to control it.

I imagine you know the feeling. And let's have some grace for ourselves, since the reason we try to control big moments is often that we care deeply.

We want the event to go smoothly.
We want the project to be a success.
We want lives to be changed.

The problem isn't that we care; the problem arises when *care* becomes *control.* That's the moment we put self back at the center of the story and try to pick up that weight only an eternal God can handle.

Maybe you resonate directly with my story. After all, revival is an amazing North Star to shoot for, and there are ways to set yourself up to experience it (prayer, fasting, worship, etc.). But the frustratingly beautiful truth is that an element of revival is completely out of our hands. Frustrating because the part of us that wants control would sure love a five-step process for revival. Beautiful because it reminds us once again that God isn't a means to an end. The breakthrough isn't the goal; God is the goal.

Sometimes breakthrough does come, but other days it doesn't. Pray for it and pursue it with shameless audacity, but practice letting go of control at the same time. Because the day you learn to surrender the outcome—and I mean really surrender (as in, still being content even when it doesn't go the way you hoped)—those walls of your me-maze will start coming down.

Chip.
Chip.
Chip.

Along the way, you just may start to notice how often God is working behind the scenes.

But there's another aspect of life **the Controller** in us tries to keep its claws in—our reputation and people's perception of us. Let's talk about that next.

4.3: I Want You to Like ~~Me~~ (You)

How to Let Go of Control in Social Situations

Jerry wanted to get clean. He wanted to get off the streets of Boulder. I knew because he told me twenty times. But he was stuck in the me-maze.

A local shelter in Boulder gives people a place to eat, sleep, and escape the cold winters. My friends and I had been leading a Bible study there every Sunday night.

"Don't just pass out brown bags," I'd been telling people. "Invite them to Bible study."

That was how we met Jerry. Over the last several months, we'd had lots of conversations with him and extended multiple invites. Each time, he'd gotten excited but then hadn't shown up.

That night, he was right on the doorstep. Literally on the doorstep of the shelter, thinking about going in.

I'd been out there with him for the better part of an hour, wishing I could somehow just show him how good a warm meal and a Bible study without judgment would be for him. But my words weren't working. Every time he started to step inside, something changed in his demeanor. He'd get mad, back up ten feet, and the chess match would start over.

I exhaled and prepared to concede defeat, assuring Jerry we could try again next week, when I heard a voice I hadn't heard in a while.

"These guys are trying to help you, Jerry." The tone was clear and confident. The type that held authority without trying to. I turned around and saw Dustin standing at the door, clean cut, completely sober, with a smile on his face. "Trust me."

His words did what mine never could.
Jerry nodded, smiled, and came inside.

I've replayed that moment a million times over the years.

Jesus told us to "love our neighbors."[1] But if you've tried, you've surely realized how challenging that can be. Because you've got your me-maze to navigate, they've got theirs, and sometimes words and actions don't get through. In those moments, resisting the temptation to make the situation about you can feel impossible. To get down on yourself when it doesn't go well and to let it stroke your ego when it does go well.

That night serves as my reminder to stop playing that game. My inner **Controller** wanted to be able to help Jerry and receive the credit that came with it. I tried everything. But in the end, it was Dustin's shot to take. He was the one with the authority, not me.

I tried for five months.
Dustin achieved success in five seconds.

And that is a beautiful truth about God's kingdom: It's upside down and illogical. It'll drive you crazy. Because when you dive deep enough into spirituality, you'll begin to see just how much is beyond our control.

Ann Landers has a brilliant line that sums up that scene on the doorstep of the shelter: "There are two kinds of people in this world. Those who walk into a room and say, 'Here I am,' and those who walk into a room and say, 'There you are.' "[2]

I showed up for Jerry, thinking, *Here I am; let me help you.* Dustin showed up for Jerry, thinking, *There you are.*

Escaping the me-maze isn't just about the inner journey of trading pressure for peace; it's about finding the freedom to show up for other people without needing anything from them. To care less about other people's perceptions. And to care more about their souls.

Social pressure is real. Especially when we get caught in the me-maze. When we put ourselves at the center of the story, we give too much weight to what people think about us. Every room we walk into becomes an audition, an opportunity to get the validation we're searching for. Our inner **Controller** sets out to control people's perception of us—performing, comparing, and avoiding anything that might detract from our self-image.

Notice the gravitational pull. When self is at the center, we pull others to us—needing something from them. But when God is at the center, we're freed up to give to others.

So we don't need to walk into a room like we're auditioning for a role as "human being." Instead, we can walk into each room on mission—knowing there are people who are hurting, lost, lonely, or just in need of someone to see them.

Life, out of the me-maze, is scandalously freeing.

We're able to show up for the Jerrys in our world without basing any of our identity on whether we'll get through to them. We're able to enjoy social interactions without overthinking each word we say. We're able to encounter opposition without getting thrown off by every critique. We're able to go through life without obsessing over people's perception of us.

Of course, on this side of eternity, we're going to get only glimpses of that freedom. But those glimpses can become more and more frequent as we practice following Jesus's call: "Whoever wants to be my disciple must deny themselves and take up their cross *daily* and follow me."[3]

Die to self. Get out of the center of the story. How often? Not once in a while. Not when it's convenient. We need to practice it *daily.*

Escaping the me-maze is a daily decision. It takes a lot of work. But it's possible. And it changes everything.

Lord, free us from us.

Remember, the goal of this book is for you to be transformed into the image of Christ. During his years of ministry, Jesus was a picture of self-giving love. Rather than performing, he'd walk into rooms and look for people to love, help, and heal. When he showed up, people were drawn to him, but he didn't use that power to search for validation for himself. Rather, he used that power as an opportunity to build others up.

Jesus was spiritual, but he didn't make spirituality about the self. What if you practiced doing the same thing today?

Here's a simple line to repeat to yourself in every social situation: *I want you to like you.*

The flesh wants to prove itself. The flesh wants to gossip to get ahead. The flesh wants to put on a show. The flesh wants your friends or family to walk away thinking about how much they like you.

When self is at the center, interactions with other people are opportunities to perform. Your flesh feels the lights come on and starts trying to show the "audience" how smart, funny, holy, or charismatic you are. But when Christ is at the center, interactions with others are opportunities to make much of *them*.

To ask really good questions about them.
To give them room to talk about whatever is going on.
To hold space for them to feel whatever they need to feel.

The anthem of the old self is, *I want you to like me.*
Flip it to, *I want you to like you.*

Try out that line. It's an easy way to flip the gravitational pull in the room. And it changes the way you interact with people.

You talk less.
You listen more.

And you begin to enjoy the scandalous freedom of God-centered spirituality.

Before we get to the end of our journey, we need to address two final spiritual practices. Both are rising in popularity, and both are examples of trying to take back the control of our own spiritual journey: psychedelics and astrology.

Let's begin with psychedelics.

4.4: Psychedelics

Why True Spirituality Requires a Long Obedience in the Same Direction

I once made up a joke. Since it's not very nice, I never say it out loud. But I feel like you and I have gotten pretty close over the course of this book, so here goes.

Q: *How do you know if someone's experienced ego death?*
A: *Don't worry—they'll tell you.*

What do you think? Pretty good, right? Obviously, it's all about the delivery. But I think it's got some potential.

If you're not familiar with it, *ego death* is a phrase some spiritual traditions use to describe dying to or transcending the self. In this context, *ego* is referring to that part of your mind that is responsible for your sense of self—your identity. So ego death is the renunciation of the need to hold on to a separate, self-centered existence.

In other words, the ego is the part of you that is trying to perform and convince the world you are enough. Ego death is self-surrender.

Although I don't use that language to describe my spiritual journey or subscribe to every belief of those who do, I think the basic concept of ego death moves in the right direction. After all, two thousand years ago, Jesus was inviting people to "deny" themselves.

Ego death is a phrase that comes up a lot when I'm talking to people about spiritual stuff. But the irony is, when they start talking about ego death, it's usually packaged in a long lecture they're giving about themselves.

"What are you working on?"

I barely heard the question over the sound of my music. But the stare coming from seat 24A was deafening. I felt like an ant scurrying off a sidewalk with a magnifying glass held over me.

Wearing AirPods on a flight should be a universal sign that you don't want to be bothered, but this guy wasn't picking up on it.

"Are you writing something?" he tried again.

"No," I said, lying through my teeth and darkening my screen.

I was determined to write.
He was determined to talk.

"I like to write myself," he said a little more loudly.

I sighed and took out my left AirPod but still held it in my hand in that passive-aggressive way we introverts use to say, "I'm working on something I'd like to continue working on, if you don't mind."

But the nonverbal cue got lost in translation, and he dove right into his story. Starting at the beginning, he told me everything that had happened to him over his twenty-four years of life.

"Uh-huh." My hopes of getting any work done dissipated with each dispensable detail.

The story was all about how he used to think he had to prove himself in every room. And then he'd gotten into psychedelics.

And then he'd *really* gotten into psychedelics. And then one night during a trip, he had an out-of-body experience when he saw a creature. The creature had told him it was his ego. And then to make a long story short, he told his ego he didn't need it anymore, and the creature shriveled up and died.

And thus—ego death.

"That's awesome, man," I said.

"It's beyond awesome," he corrected. Then he explained how ever since that moment he no longer needed to prove himself. "I used to obsess over getting other people's approval, but now I couldn't care less."

Great, so I can get back to my writing?

No such luck.

From there, he told me about everything he'd been able to accomplish since transcending his ego, and then the plane landed.

That was the moment I made up the joke in my mind.

If you think it's mean, don't worry. The only ones who could ever be offended by it technically can't be offended, because their ego is dead. Which I guess makes it the perfect joke. But it does highlight a pattern I believe needs to be called out.

You'd think an experience that allows someone to transcend themselves would move them to talk about themselves *less,* not *more.* Although that may be the case sometimes, I have a lot of personal data to suggest that when the experience involves psychedelics, that's usually not how it goes.

As a pastor in Austin, I get asked my opinion about the intersection of psychedelics and spirituality all the time. Let me begin by stating the obvious: I'm not a doctor. I know nothing about the pros or cons of psychedelics with health issues like chronic pain. My opinion in that regard shouldn't hold any water, so I'll spare you. This isn't me trying to turn into some professional. This is me being a pastor, reporting on what I've observed from watching others attempt to use psychedelics to aid in spirituality.

Psychedelics and Spirituality

When people explain their psychedelic experiences to me (at least the positive ones), it often sounds like they're getting a temporary version of what we've been talking about in this book.

The positive experiences typically seem to involve their old self, or their flesh, taking a break. As though psychedelics allow them to get out of the center of the story and stop feeling the need to perform or compare for a moment. Which, as we've discovered, otherwise takes a lot of work. It's no wonder psychedelics are becoming so popular.

Psilocybin retreats.
Ketamine therapy.[1]
Ayahuasca ceremonies.

I have friends who rave about them. As though they are shortcuts out of the me-maze. So, the million-dollar question: Should psychedelics be part of our self-less spirituality journey?

They aren't part of mine.
For two primary reasons.

Reason 1

The first is simple: Just because something is spiritual doesn't mean it's good. After all, there is a very real enemy who is also spiritual.

For every story I hear about how a psychedelic experience was helpful for someone, I watch four or five other people lose themselves along the way, becoming less grounded in reality.

Imagine a balloon on a string, with the string representing the idea of being grounded in our current reality, and the balloon representing the truth that we are part of an eternal story.

During his ministry, Jesus was a picture of both string and balloon. He was a normal human grounded on the earth who hung out with other people (string). But he was also deeply connected to heaven and able to bring people back from the dead (balloon). He was "in the world (string) but not of the world (balloon)."

But we're not Jesus, so the balance can be a challenge. It's easy to become all string and no balloon—where we have theological and intellectual answers for everything but very little experience to go with it. And it's equally easy to become all balloon and no string—where everything is about an emotive experience and we lose our ability to have normal conversations in everyday life.

I've watched several people add psychedelics to the mix only to lose the string along the way. Conversations with them become cloudy. As though there's a loss of logic and common sense. They're like balloons floating around up in the rafters, going into great detail about what they've seen and how much more enlightened they are than those who still have an ego.

By the way, as a general rule, when your spiritual experience makes you feel superior to others, you should reevaluate the path you're on. If you catch yourself spouting self-centered anthems like, "Well, you don't really get it," or "You haven't experienced it like I have," you might be falling into a false spirituality.

After all, Jesus never said anything like that. He did the opposite. He made room for everyone at the table. He didn't make others feel spiritually inferior; he just invited them into the experience. In fact, the only people he had strong words for were the Pharisees, Sadducees, and scribes who did think they were further along than others.

Jesus is a brilliant picture of both balloon and string. On the journey of being renewed in his image, cutting the string is a step in the wrong direction.

Reason 2

Psychedelics also aren't in my spiritual toolbox because of what I've noticed repeatedly in the lives of those who do subscribe to them. Even if some of the experiences are positive (and I'm very skeptical they are), the results are only temporary.

No work is required to get there.
And that's a recipe for disaster.

To explain what I mean, let's use a more concrete example—money.

One of the most famous stories Jesus ever told is often called the parable of the Prodigal Son. It's about a son who asked his father for his inheritance early, but when his father gave it to him, he went off and "squandered his wealth in wild living."[2]

When he came to his senses, he returned home expecting to be punished, but instead, his father ran to him, embraced him, and threw him a party.

It's an epic story, with countless takeaways about God's radical love and the power of repentance. But somewhere down near the bottom of a long list of lessons is a simple observation: What tends to happen when someone gets their hands on a lot of money—that they didn't earn—way too early?

Most of the time, they squander it.

Why? Because building wealth requires years of hard work and wise decisions. That hard work and those wise decisions are like going to the gym. They help you build up the muscles you need to handle the money when you acquire it. The principles are supposed to be implemented before the result.

But if you get the money without building up the muscles needed to handle that kind of wealth, you don't know how to sustain it.

One of the reasons I've filled this book with stories of my own failed attempts to take self out of the center is that I want you to see the journey. I'm in the middle of the process, but I'm working on it. And along the way, that spiritual muscle is getting stronger. By God's grace, I'm getting better at taking self out of the center and am working out the spiritual muscles needed to keep it that way.

It seems to me, psychedelics create the experience without developing the spiritual muscles needed to sustain the results. It's like being given a fortune without implementing wise financial practices.

Does a person who uses psychedelics escape the me-maze for a moment? Maybe. But even if they do, they don't know how to do it again without the drug. So, they're doomed to keep going back to the drug to get what they want. In other words, psychedelics do what every other drug does: They get you right to the brink of what you're looking for, but instead of leaving you there, they pull you away and remind you you're now dependent on them to get what you want.

When people ask me about psychedelics, they're often shocked I don't participate. As though I'm not a real spiritual seeker if I'm not willing to use shortcuts. But I reject the notion that you're missing out on God unless you use supplements.

Spiritual experiences are available and ready for us to step into. But getting there requires a lot of silence, stillness, Scripture, honesty, confession, forgiveness, fasting, patience, and usually pain. But the beauty for those who are willing to play the long game is that we can continue to move away from self-centered spirituality and into Christ-centered spirituality without needing assistance from a substance.

To me, that's a vision worth chasing. Because that sounds like freedom.

A Long Obedience in the Same Direction

I was frustrated on my drive home from the airport. I had a deadline coming up, and instead of getting any writing done, I'd had to listen to some guy's rant about his ego death.

But eventually, frustration gave way to curiosity. I started thinking about how many people are going down that path, using psychedelics while the world cheers them on, with seemingly no warning about the deep, dense me-maze the drugs thrust them into.

When I got home, a box was waiting for me on my front porch. I opened the package to find a book so well crafted that it gave me the answer I was searching for right in the title: *A Long Obedience in the Same Direction* by Eugene Peterson.

From the very first page, Peterson took on the role of mentor, saying, "One aspect of *world* that I have been able to identify as harmful to Christians is the assumption that anything worthwhile can be acquired at once."[3]

It was like he understood my rising frustration with quick-fix spirituality hacks. And he offered another option. He quoted Friedrich Nietzsche—who, for all his wild thoughts, was spot on with this spiritual truth: "The essential thing 'in heaven and earth' is . . . that there should be long obedience in the same direction."[4]

The funny thing is, the first edition of Peterson's book was published in 1980. Even back then, Peterson was already pointing out, "Our attention spans have been conditioned by thirty-second commercials. Our sense of reality has been flattened by thirty-page abridgments."[5]

Today thirty-second commercials are the least of our worries. And most people consider it a win if they can get through a "thirty-page abridgment." Our attention spans have gotten significantly worse, and it's greatly affecting our spirituality. Peterson's prophetic warning has proved hauntingly accurate. (By the way, great job getting all the way to the end of this book. Don't tell anyone, but I saved the best chapters for last.)

Over the next few nights, I dove deep into Peterson's book, which walks through the Songs of Ascent (Psalms 120–34) and shows how they are an invitation to stop being a tourist and become a pilgrim. A tourist, in this sense, is one who shows up to the attractive areas of religion when it's convenient for them, mostly to take pictures. But pilgrims, on the other hand, are "people who spend our lives going someplace, going to God, and whose path for getting there is the way, Jesus Christ. We realize that 'this world is not my home' and set out for 'the Father's house.' "[6]

That was what I wanted to help the extrovert on the plane see.

Psychedelics can only help us be spiritual tourists. We show up, take some pictures, and then leave. But if we want to be pilgrims, we can't take shortcuts. We have to devote our lives to following the way of Jesus, with a long obedience.

That was what God was speaking to me that day when I was ironically being a tourist in New York City.

Free me from me isn't a prayer you can pray once to check off a box. It's a lifelong journey, which is frustrating in the age of instant gratification. But if we can persevere beyond the anxious shallow waters, we can begin to see the beautiful invitation into something much more sacred than short-term change. The offer is a deep, heart-level transformation that comes as a result of communing with the Creator of the universe daily.

Fitness gurus know getting in shape is about making healthy decisions *daily.*
Finance whizzes know acquiring wealth is about making wise financial decisions *daily.*

The same thing is true here. This prayer is about surrendering your own agenda, your own desires, your own bitterness toward those who have stepped on you in the past, and all the other games the old self used to play, and taking up your cross *daily.* It doesn't happen overnight, and there is no super-secret formula you can use.

The Performer in us doesn't like that, because it wants validation and it wants it now. **The Comparer** in us doesn't like that, because that process feels too slow to keep up with the competition. **The Avoider** in us just wants to reach a destination already. And **the Controller** in us despises all of this talk about surrender.

Our flesh doesn't like a long obedience.
But a long obedience allows our souls to come alive.

Psychedelics are an attempt to cut in line and expedite the results. To be a spiritual tourist who gets their picture taken next to "enlightenment" even though they don't have any ability to return to it until their next vacation. It goes against the grain of God's design for spirituality and pushes us deeper into the me-maze.

The real trail can be grueling, but the view is phenomenal, and the company is good. It's full of pilgrims who have all discovered in their own way that there is no super-secret formula. There is no drug we can take or ceremony we can attend.

The only way forward is a long obedience in the same direction.

4.5: Astrology

What's Really Written in the Stars?

The sky was losing light quickly. Our whole staff was standing on the roof of the church, looking up through our super-slick eclipse-themed glasses as the moon crept farther over the sun.

Even though a total solar eclipse happens somewhere on earth every eighteen months, it happens in a single location only once every 375 years.[1] But on April 8, 2024, Austin happened to be in the path of totality (the new phrase we'd all just learned but were pretending like we'd known all along), so we climbed a sketchy ladder to our roof to watch.

Sure enough, at 1:36 P.M., just as the experts had told us, the city went dark. The moon completely covered the sun, and it might as well have been nighttime in the middle of the afternoon.

I looked around the city.
It was a really cool moment.
And, if I'm being honest, a little strange.
And just a tiny bit scary.

Which may sound funny, because I knew what was happening. We had the explanation. But still, it was a little unnerving.

Imagine you're a farmer living thousands of years ago and that same event took place, except without any warning. No explanation. No fancy new phrases. No glasses. All you know is it's nighttime when it's supposed to be day, and you have no clue if it'll ever end. That would be downright terrifying.

Once it did end, you might not be able to help but wonder what it meant. Was it an omen? Was an enemy nation about to attack you? Was your king about to die? Was a famine coming?

You wouldn't know. And you would desperately want to find out.

I say all that to say this: It makes complete sense that astrology ("the study of movements and relative positions of celestial bodies interpreted as having an influence on human affairs and the natural world"[2]) has been around for thousands of years. As mysterious as the world still is to us today, imagine it before we had any explanations.

Ancient Astrology

Humans are meaning makers—we can't help but look for explanations to mysteries. It's our attempt to try to control the uncontrollable.

The Babylonians (as we find out in the book of Daniel) were all about this. They had a collection of about seventy tablets called *Enūma Anu Enlil* chock-full of observations about the stars, sun, moon, and planets and what they believed it all meant for them. Most of it was linked to their survival (and the survival of the king).[3] When the king had a big decision to make or a dream that was bothering him, he would turn to the text and the astrologers for answers.

In Daniel 2, Daniel was living as an exile in Babylon and King Nebuchadnezzar was having sleep problems. His dreams were keeping him up at night. So he called in the astrologers to give him the interpretation of his latest dream.

In short, it didn't go well. They answered the king, "There is no one on earth who can do what the king asks! No king, however great and mighty, has ever asked such a thing of any magician or enchanter or astrologer. What the king asks is too difficult. No one can reveal it to the king except the gods, and they do not live among humans."[4]

As you can imagine, Nebuchadnezzar was less than thrilled with that answer: "This made the king so furious that he ordered the execution of all the wise men of Babylon."[5]

Have I mentioned self-centered spirituality comes with unrelenting pressure?

Eventually, Daniel was brought into the equation and wisely explained, "No wise man, enchanter, magician or diviner can explain to the king the mystery he has asked about, but there is a God in heaven who reveals mysteries."[6]

In other words, self-centered spirituality wasn't going to work here.

Daniel's entire life is a fascinating case study of staying obedient to God-centered spirituality while living as an exile in a land of people entrenched in their self-centered spirituality practices. His story is a gift for us in the twenty-first century.

My qualm really isn't with ancient Babylonian astrologers. They seem to have been spiritual seekers doing their best, and if you know your Bible, you know that, six hundred years later, "wise men from the east" would follow a star to a baby named Jesus.[7]

They were looking up into the sky.
And God met them where they were.
He used the sky to point them to Jesus.

But when people bring up astrology today, they aren't talking about wise men from the east doing their best; they are referring to the multi-billion-dollar industry that has been built around astrology.

Astrology Today

In 2024, a poll given to more than two thousand U.S. adults found that 70 percent believe in astrology and 29 percent pay monthly for astrological services.[8] Even more sobering, as many as seventy million Americans read their horoscope daily.[9] Which is a bummer because only sixty-three million Americans report engaging with the Bible at least weekly.[10]

Did you catch that? More Americans read their horoscope than their Bible.

In 2021, astrology was a $12.8 billion industry. That number is expected to be $22.8 billion by 2031.[11]

To me, astrology is the clearest picture of the rise of spirituality that centers on the self.

Think about it. How are they able to put up numbers that big? The answer is so simple that every marketer knows it: You just have to appeal to the me-maze. Create a spiritual practice that encourages people to stay at the center of their own universe, and they will hand you their credit card.

Where church is a family that invites you to be part of the bigger story, astrology puts you at the center of the story. In modern astrology, you are the star of the show, and the night sky is here to give you answers about you. It takes the vastness of the night sky and the magnificence of the moon, the stars, and the planets and asks, "What does all this say about me?"

Astrology is a brilliant system that traps people in the me-maze by offering us two things we all want—a way to be seen and a method to hold on to control.

Astrology and Control

Let's be really honest about why astrology is rising in popularity: It gives answers. And in a scary world that is full of mystery and questions, answers are incredibly appealing.

But "certainty" is seductive.

Of course, air quotes are needed around "certainty" because the answers astrology gives are just created by humans. Nonetheless, they're still answers. Plus, astrology doesn't just give answers to any old questions; it gives answers to the most frustrating questions.

Why do you think horoscopes revolve around romantic relationships, personality insights, and major life decisions? Because those are the big questions everyone is asking.

Love is incredibly risky. It's two imperfect people trusting each other with the most vulnerable pieces of themselves. When it works out, it's incredible. When it doesn't, it's excruciating.

Love is frightening, fun, and anxiety inducing all at once. In its early stages, romance brings up a whole bunch of questions, and astrology swoops in with all the answers—offering certainty in the midst of uncertainty.

It's really painful to go through a breakup with someone you truly loved. It's a lot easier to go through that breakup when you know it wasn't a good fit because you're a Gemini and they're a Scorpio.

Astrology offers answers. A way to control the narrative as you traverse the difficult terrain of life. The problem is, it pushes you further and further into the me-maze in the process.

So What's Really Written in the Stars?

The stars have a purpose, and David, the poet and giant-killer, sang all about it one night as he peered up into the night sky:

"The heavens declare the glory of God; the skies proclaim the work of his hands."[12]

When David looked up into the night sky, he was led to worship the One who created it all. When we look up into the night sky, we wonder if we are compatible with someone who was born in October. Do you see the difference?

One is God-centered.
The other is self-centered.

Lord, free us from us.

Astrology is a phenomenal picture of the difference between self-centered spirituality and Christ-centered spirituality. And of course it's on the rise, because it's the natural outworking of the me-maze. The more we convince ourselves that we are at the center of the story, the more we'll interpret stars as messengers sent to tell us about *us.* Astrology allows us to be obsessed with self rather than worshipping the One who hung the constellations in the night sky.

The irony is, the comfort and peace we are hoping to get out of astrology are actually found in worship. In taking ourselves out of the center of the story and putting God there.

Astrology will always leave you needing more astrology. Putting unrelenting pressure on your shoulders.

Another night, David looked up at the stars and sang:

> When I consider your heavens,
> the work of your fingers,
> the moon and the stars,
> which you have set in place,
> what is mankind that you are mindful of them,
> human beings that you care for them?[13]

David spent a lot of time stargazing, so we should, too. But when David looked at the stars, he was moved to ask this question: *Who am I that you are mindful of me?* Stars reminded him just how big and beautiful the God at the center of the story is. And in return, it filled him with awe that God also cared deeply about him.

These days, here's the version of Psalm 8:3–4 I feel we're living out:

> *When I consider your heavens,*
> *the work of your fingers,*
> *the moon and the stars,*
> *which you have set in place,*
> *I wonder what they are trying to tell me about me.*

When you put yourself at the center of the story, it makes sense that you would look up into the night sky and wonder if that's why you're feeling *off* today.

But when God is at the center of the story, you can look up and feel awe and wonder at the vast goodness of the One who created it all. And then you'll eventually join in with David and feel overwhelmingly grateful that the same star-breathing Creator doesn't just know who you are but also genuinely cares about you.

Letting the night sky tell us why we're feeling how we're feeling is rising in popularity, but let me offer another option—an ancient option: Let the night sky remind you that God sees and loves you.

That big meeting you have coming up . . . the Creator of the universe knows all about it and cares deeply.
That intimidating conversation you have tomorrow . . . the Creator of the universe knows all about it and cares deeply.

That painful breakup you are going through . . . the Creator of the universe knows all about it and cares deeply.

God sees you.
God loves you.
God is with you.

And God-centered spirituality is scandalously freeing.

4.6: All the Known You Need

A Saying That'll Free You from You

"Is fame all it's cracked up to be?"[1]

The interviewer was Gabe Lyons, the founder of THINQ—a media company that hosts a conference about the intersection of faith and culture in Nashville every year.

I love going to this conference—think TED Talks for Christians (and add in lots of good coffee and fedoras)—but I wasn't at this one. I was watching a clip from my bedroom. My book was coming out in two weeks and sales were up and down.

I was spiraling again.
I didn't want to be.
I didn't mean to be.

But I was.

I could preach myself out of the spiral on the good days, but this was a bad day. The flesh had come to play. It was calling the shots and didn't seem all that interested in any of the positive self-talk I was throwing at it to silence it.

It wasn't a book sale crisis.
It was an existential crisis.

I did all this work because I thought the payoff would be better. But here we are. Some people are going to read the book—great. But I'm still insecure.

The fig leaves weren't nearly as big as I thought they'd be.

You know you're in a bad place when you're turning to YouTube for help. But Gabe's thumbnail had caught my attention. He's always been good at asking the questions we're all thinking about, and this was certainly one of them: "Is fame all it's cracked up to be?"

"Everyone wants to be known," responded Tony Hale, a talented actor I knew best as the beloved Buster Bluth on one of my favorite shows—*Arrested Development*. "And they look at fame as the ultimate being known," he continued with a much more serious tone than I was used to from him. He talked about how the common belief is that if we get lots of followers on Twitter or Instagram, it will convert to being fully known.

"Exactly," my flesh said out loud.

And then he dropped this line: "But the thing is, if you're known by people you love, that's all the known you need."

The words jumped over all the protective barriers my old self had put up, edged past the guards, and struck a chord in some deep piece of my soul. The place buried by my anxious attempt to promote myself.

All the *known* you *need.*

He went on to talk about how isolating fame can be because it can be hard to trust people's intentions. And how some guy working a nine-to-five and then going home to his family can actually be way more known than the famous person who lives in isolation.

As he talked, I started to see just how much of my effort is an attempt to be known.

Maybe you know the feeling.

Whether it's followers, influence, money, or power, you likely have something you pour much of your time and attention into. But just how deep a breath could you take if you realized you've already got all the known you need?

To Tony Hale's point, having a few people in your life who truly know you is all the known you need. And to add to that thought, being known by your Creator is all the known you need.

Jeremiah 1:5 says, "Before I formed you in the womb I knew you."

God knows you. If you have a relationship with the Creator of the universe where you are actively surrendering to love and placing him back at the center of the story—*that's all the known you need.*

Numbers on social media may be important for your career, but they aren't a good indicator of your level of known-ness.

Paul urged us to "carry each other's burdens, and in this way you will fulfill the law of Christ."[2]

But people can't carry your burdens if they don't know what they are. We search for being known in so many silly ways, but if you have a few people in your life who know the real you—*that's all the known you need.*

Try the line out. Next time you open social media and feel that despair because you lost some followers, speak this over yourself:

I've got all the known I need.
When you put yourself out there but get rejected—*I've got all the known I need.*
When you get caught in the comparison trap by seeing someone do the same thing as you but get more notoriety for it—*I've got all the known I need.*

The flesh wants validation. And to get it, it's willing to promote itself however it can. But the spirit knows the truth. The spirit knows that it's all just fig leaves. That God sees you for who you really are and that if you can be real with a few people, they will see you as you really are.

If you can just make that your focus, it won't take long to realize you *are* known by a few people—*and that's all the known you need.*

Why do people turn to psychedelics to enhance their spiritual experience? For some extra help? To save some time? To turn up the knob? Sure. But at the deepest level, it seems to me that people do that because they don't actually know that God loves them just how they are—*and that's all the known they need.*

Why do people spend billions on astrology? Because they're desperate for answers and control? Sure. But at the deepest level, it's because they don't fully trust that they're known by the One who hung the constellations in the night sky—*and that's all the known they need.*

The final layer of the me-maze is the most stubborn. The wall of control doesn't go down without a fight. But what's waiting on the other side is the deep knowledge that you are created in the image of God. That you are fully known and truly loved by the One who made you—*and that's all the known you need.*

Chip.
Chip.
Chip.

Everything from this season of my life—from learning to preach without panicking, to handling the pandemic, to releasing my first book, to being a tourist in New York—comes down to understanding that I already have all the known I need.

And it all came to a head one night on the Nāpali Coast.

4.7: The Necessary Tension

How to Find the Scandalous Freedom of Trust in an Age of Control

The Nāpali Coast is one of my favorite places on this planet. It's on the northwest side of Kauai and isn't easy to get to. Fortunately, my good friends Matt and Jess live there and let me spend a week with them every summer.

One summer, Matt and I decided to kayak along the entire Nāpali Coast. Jess dropped us off on the north side of the island with a kayak, spearguns, and some food in case the spearfishing didn't pan out (it didn't) and promised to pick us up on the northwest side of the island three days later.

On the second day, we put in at an empty beach. There was nothing we had to do.
And nowhere we had to be.
Our phones were off. And wouldn't have had service anyway.
It was a deep exhale.

Matt spent the entire afternoon out on the water, trying to catch dinner. I joined him for the first hour, then decided the Easy Mac we'd brought would suffice. So after leaving Matt to it, I sat on the beach with my journal and stared out at the endless sea, my hand gripping my pen as I scribbled away about everything that had happened in the last few years.

Planting a church with my friends.
Leading through a pandemic.
Learning how to quiet **the Performer** and preach without the spiral.

Putting out my first book after spending four years of my life working on it (the book had been out for two months at that point, and **the Comparer** in me still checked the Amazon rankings more than I cared to admit).
Pastoring in Austin, Texas, where everyone is open to spirituality but often allergic to big truth statements. Where everyone loves Jesus but calls you closed minded when you teach what Jesus actually said. Where it's so easy for me to avoid conflict and shrink back instead of sharing the wisdom I know I need to share.
Shepherding people in an age when credibility is based off the number of followers you have. And followers are typically based off charisma. So person after person has a story of their own "spiritual" experiences where the influencer promised so much freedom but left them feeling so much bondage.

My journal was hearing all about it.

Finally, one word emerged above the rest. The word I'd been chasing for years—from the busy streets of Manhattan to the remote beaches of Kauai. Writing story after story in my journal along the way, until I finally saw it:

Pressure.

I'm putting so much pressure on myself. Pressure to have this whole life thing figured out. Pressure to then put simple language to it and explain it to everyone else.

Once I saw it, it seemed so obvious. But I guess I had to go through all that to get there. It was like I finally removed myself from the center of the story long enough to see it. I was weary and burdened because I'd forgotten there was already a hero to this story—his name is Jesus, and he's a lot better at handling the pressure than I am.

"I got one," Matt said, getting out of the water as the sun began to set.
"Yes!" I said, reaching for the knife in our backpack.
"*Got* one," he clarified. "I didn't say I have one. It got away."
"Probably for the best," I assured him. "I'm not really in the mood for fresh fish."
"Yeah, Easy Mac just sounded better," he said, smiling.

Matt's a therapist, a really good one. He knows how to read people and was more than aware that I hadn't quite been myself all week.

We'd talked through it all.
The book.
The church.
All the questions about God I thought I was supposed to have answers to.
All the ways I turn spirituality into a performance, the ways writing turns me into a comparer, and the way all of that makes me just want to avoid everything and everyone because this whole journey has thrown me right back into the me-maze.

All week, Matt had challenged me to pick a word for what I was feeling, to name it. And until that moment, I'd drawn a blank.

"I know the word," I told him. He stared off into the water, no doubt thinking about all the fish who'd spent their afternoon outsmarting him. "The word is *pressure*. . . . It's like I put an unrelenting, never-ending amount of pressure on my shoulders."

The mac 'n' cheese was ready, and dusk was settling in as the first stars emerged. I poured the remains of the water we'd filtered from the stream behind our campsite into two cups and handed him one.

"I get that," he eventually said. "I feel it, too. Sometimes I get scared of mediocrity."

"What do you mean?" I asked.

"Part of me feels like it's a sin to play small with all the gifts God's given me," he explained. "I think that's why I put so much pressure on myself."

We sat in silence for a few minutes, enjoying our dinner. Reality sinking in that we had nowhere to be and that there was no shot clock on our conversation.

"I googled it once," Matt said.

"What?"

"Yeah, I googled 'Is it a sin to be average?' "

We both laughed.

"What'd you find?" I asked.

"The cobbler in Corinth," he said as more stars began popping up in the night sky.

I started thinking through Paul's letters to Corinth, inwardly panicking that I'd missed the verse about the cobbler.

"It's just a story," Matt said (a therapist's way of telling a pastor to relax). "We always hear about the high-level leaders Paul built up along the way. Like Timothy and Silas, who join him on his epic adventures. But what if there was a guy who was just a faithful cobbler in Corinth? Who started following the way of Jesus and then stayed where he was. And ran his shop with integrity and loved his wife really well and stuff—not every act of faithfulness makes the news."[1]

Something about the story felt freeing.

It was spirituality without all the pressure.

By that point, an unbelievable number of stars painted the sky.

We were miles away from the nearest hint of light pollution.

It was the type of night I imagine Abraham experienced when God said, “Look up at the sky and count the stars—if indeed you can count them.”[2]

We walked to the water’s edge and stood where the small waves crashed. The Pacific Ocean looked so peaceful in the moment, though I knew from the day’s adventures that was a façade.

Then I nearly fell over when I looked up. Earlier the trees had been blocking half the sky, but down by the water, we had a full view of thousands of stars.

We stood in awe for the better part of an hour.
No words exchanged.
None needed.

I thought about all the pressure I put on myself.
And how I’d turned spirituality into a means to an end.
And how appealing being a cobbler in Corinth sounded.

I realized how I was slowly developing a deep trust for the God who knows me. A trust that wasn’t built overnight but is the result of a lot of honest prayers, difficult conversations, panic attacks in Manhattan, awkward self-centered worship nights, early mornings caught in the comparison trap, failed attempts to atone for my own sin, and a loving Father who has been there every step of the way, patiently inviting me into a long obedience in the same direction.

Psalm 8 ran through my mind:

When I consider your heavens,
the work of your fingers,
the moon and the stars,
which you have set in place,
what is mankind that you are mindful of them,
human beings that you care for them?[3]

The One who hangs constellations in the night sky is mindful of me. He cares for me. Not some future version of me who better reflects his image—the me right here and now.

I opened my hands in front of me, palms facing the ground like I was letting go of everything I was holding, and *exhaled.* At the end of the exhale, I realized it was time for another inhale—literally and figuratively. I realized there's a reason I'm here, that this God who I genuinely trust is at work in my life and is calling me to be at work in this world, and thought about the next lines of the psalm:

You have made them a little lower than the angels
and crowned them with glory and honor.
You made them rulers over the works of your hands;
you put everything under their feet.[4]

You and I were created on purpose for a purpose. God created us to rule in this world, calling us to be his image bearers on this earth.

I flipped my hands over, palms now facing the sky like I was ready to receive, and *inhaled.*

In his brilliant book, *The Winding Path of Transformation,* my friend and mentor Jeff Tacklind writes about those earlier lines of Psalm 8 and the vastness of God's creation: "My egocentric little world collapses at that image," he says. "I realize I'm not that important. That life is not about me."[5]

But then the psalmist explained God crowning us "with glory and honor," and Jeff notes, "It is paradoxical. Humanity is both majestic and insignificant. We live in the place of both glory and humility. It is a necessary tension."[6]

Necessary tension is a great phrase. The only way to get out (and stay out) from under the unrelenting pressure of self-centeredness is to realize this paradox: You have an important role, but God's at the center—you are majestic and insignificant at the same time.

Surrender Breath Prayer

So, to end, one final breath prayer. This time adding in the hand motions. On the inhale, put your hands out in front of you (palms facing the sky) to receive the honor of being an image bearer. On the exhale, flip your hands over (palms facing the ground) and let go of thinking you're all that important.

Inhale: God, I'm made in your image.
Exhale: Free me from me.

Inhale for five seconds.
Exhale for five seconds.
Do this fifteen times.

If you made it through all fifteen rounds, you're probably feeling something similar to what I felt that night in Kauai—gratitude.

I kept breathing as the waves crashed gently over my feet, feeling so grateful that the God who created it all knows the real me, cares about my well-being, and truly loves me not for what I bring to the table but just for who I am.

The same is true about you. When you take self out of the center of the story, you start to realize God's love is contingent not on what you do but on who you are.

I'm grateful for friendships like the one I have with Matt, where I can be truly known. For decades, we've had these talks where we try to figure out the world, and we may not be any closer to cracking the code, but it's sure fun to try. There's an immense freedom to those conversations once you take yourself out of the center. Like a subtle nod from God, an invitation on every inhale to keep trying, thinking, and talking—but then on each exhale to let go and appreciate the mystery of it all.

I lowered my gaze to the ocean, peering as far out as my eyes would let me. More lines from David popped into my head: "By the word of the LORD the heavens were made, their starry host by the breath of his mouth. He gathers the waters of the sea into jars."[7]

From the immeasurable heights of the starry sky.
To the unfathomable depths of the sea.

The One who made it all is inviting us out of the maze of self-centeredness.

For a moment, I realized I was experiencing what I hope you've been feeling as you read this book. I wasn't thinking about my insecurities; I wasn't trying to perform; I wasn't caught in the comparison trap; I wasn't running away from the present moment; I wasn't trying to control any of it.

I was free from me, enjoying the scandalous freedom of trusting that God is at the center of all of this.

And it finally felt like rest for my weary soul.

It's such a simple idea.

Some call it dangerous.
Others say preposterous.
Most don't give it a second thought.

But as I hope you're starting to see, this simple idea has the potential to change everything about your life.

Lord, free me from me.

Acknowledgments

This project took me on a long, rigorous, and sometimes scary journey. Words cannot express how grateful I am that I had so many people walking with me along the way.

Matt Fons: For all the adventures, conversations, and encouragement you gave me to write this one. This book would not exist without you.

Beej Bartolome: For that walk through Central Park that inspired this book and for always being in my corner.

Ethan and Stef Matott: For that dinner where I pitched this idea. You were the first ones to hear it. Thank you for seeing and calling out its potential.

Doug and Sam Wekenman: For always giving me space to process all my ideas and for inspiring me to keep writing.

Mom and Dad: For all the long walks and conversations we had about this book along the way.

Shawn Johnson: For being such an amazing pastor and for teaching me how to write about the real stuff.

Red Rocks Church: For all the encouragement to continue pressing into this topic and write this book. I love that we get to change the world together!

Kyle Negrete: For always calling out potential in me.

Keith Garton: For your brilliant notes during that breakfast at that diner.

Jeff Tacklind: For all the Spiritual Direction sessions that permeate these pages.

Kory Miller: For helping me brainstorm a thousand different titles.

Brinnae Keathley: For all the conversations about theology, creativity, and the image of God.

A. J. Norman: For all the brilliant marketing ideas.

Greg and Jenna Lewis: For all the theological conversations and support. And for encouraging me to keep writing that one night when I was ready to give up.

Kevin Reddington: For all your notes, text messages, and thoughtful insights about God, the self, and spirituality.

Brett and Allie Crews: For reading early drafts and helping me figure out what I really wanted to say.

Oliver Drewes: For all the Friday morning workouts that turned into pep talks to finish the book.

Johnny Shinnick: For creating artwork for those early versions of the me-maze. I stared at them as I wrote so much of this book.

Matt and Regan Zuege: For all the dinners where you encouraged me to keep writing.

Leslie Calhoun: For believing in this book and helping me bring it to life with all your thoughtful ideas and edits.

The entire WaterBrook team: For working so hard to make this book matter.

Notes

Lord, Free Me from Me

1. Matthew 11:28.

Introduction: From Self-Centered to God-Centered

1. Wim Hof, "Wim Hof Breathing Tutorial," YouTube, September 28, 2018, 10 min., 7 sec., youtube.com/watch?v=nzCaZQqAs9I&t=186s.
2. Legend says that Copernicus woke up from a coma, held his book, and died peacefully.
3. To be fair, a Greek astronomer named Aristarchus of Samos proposed this idea about 1,700 years earlier. But Copernicus was the first to move beyond speculation and explain it with a scientific framework.
4. Genesis 1:1.
5. 2 Timothy 3:2–4.
6. Colossians 3:9–10.
7. Steven R. Guthrie, *Creator Spirit: The Holy Spirit and the Art of Becoming Human* (Baker Academic, 2011), xvi.

1.1: The Me-Maze (Part 1)

1. Genesis 2:7.
2. Genesis 2:7.

1.2: The Spotlight Effect

1. Romans 8:5.
2. Thomas Gilovich, Victoria Husted Medvec, and Kenneth Savitsky, "The Spotlight Effect in Social Judgment: An Egocentric Bias in Estimates of the Salience of One's Own Actions and Appearance," *Journal of Personality and Social Psychology* 78, no. 2 (2000): 211–22, doi.org/10.1037/0022-3514.78.2.211.
3. Thomas Gilovich and Kenneth Savitsky, "The Spotlight Effect and the Illusion of Transparency: Egocentric Assessments of How We Are Seen by Others," *Current Directions in Psychological Science* 8, no. 6 (1999): 165–68, doi.org/10.1111/1467-8721.00039.
4. Genesis 3:4.

5. Genesis 3:5.
6. John 8:44.
7. Christopher A. Hall, "Reading Christ into the Heart: The Theological Foundations of *Lectio Divina*," in *Life in the Spirit: Spiritual Formation in Theological Perspective*, ed. Jeffrey P. Greenman and George Kalantzis (IVP Academic, 2010), 148.
8. Genesis 3:7.
9. Genesis 3:9–10.
10. Genesis 3:10.
11. C. S. Lewis, in "Reflections: The 'Hydra' of Pride," C. S. Lewis Institute, March 1, 2015, cslewisinstitute.org/resources/reflections-march-2015.

1.3: The Problem with Being the One in Charge

1. Carl R. Trueman, *Strange New World: How Thinkers and Activists Redefined Identity and Sparked the Sexual Revolution* (Crossway, 2022), 46.
2. Charles Taylor, *A Secular Age* (The Belknap Press of Harvard University Press, 2007), 473.
3. Matthew 7:24–27.

1.4: Worship

1. Matthew 11:28.
2. Timothy Keller (@timkellernyc), "Worship is an act of ascribing ultimate value to something or someone in a way that engages your entire being," X, August 7, 2014, x.com/timkellernyc/status/497351543235309569.
3. G. K. Beale, *We Become What We Worship: A Biblical Theology of Idolatry* (IVP Academic, 2008), 222.
4. Genesis 2:20.
5. Genesis 2:15.
6. 1 Corinthians 10:31.
7. Matthew 4:1.
8. Matthew 4:9.
9. Matthew 4:10.

1.5: Image of God

1. Genesis 2:7.
2. 1 John 4:19.
3. Ephesians 1:11.
4. Romans 8:37.
5. Ephesians 1:5.

6. Steven R. Guthrie, *Creator Spirit: The Holy Spirit and the Art of Becoming Human* (Baker Academic, 2011), 42.
7. Owen Strachan, *Reenchanting Humanity: A Theology of Mankind* (Mentor, 2019), 22.
8. Genesis 1:26, NLT.
9. G. K. Beale, *The Temple and the Church's Mission: A Biblical Theology of the Dwelling Place of God* (IVP Academic, 2004), 82.
10. Genesis 1:28.
11. Romans 3:23.
12. 1 John 2:2.
13. Colossians 1:15.
14. M. R. Mulholland and R. R. Barton, *Invitation to a Journey: A Road Map for Spiritual Formation* (InterVarsity Press, 2016), 12.
15. "Son of Man," BibleProject, bibleproject.com/videos/son-of-man.

1.6: Breath Prayer

1. Some names throughout the book have been changed to protect the identities and privacy of those mentioned.
2. Isaiah 42:5.
3. Philip Jenkins, *The Lost History of Christianity: The Thousand-Year Golden Age of the Church in the Middle East, Africa, and Asia—and How It Died* (HarperOne, 2008), 198.
4. Luke 18:13.
5. Mark 10:47.
6. There have been several versions of this prayer, but each one gets at the same thing: repentance.
7. 1 Thessalonians 5:17, ESV.
8. Colossians 3:16.
9. Matthew 6:7, NKJV.
10. Matthew 6:6.
11. Hebrews 4:12.

1.7: Let It Die

1. David Augsburger, *Caring Enough to Hear and Be Heard* (Regal, 1982), 12.

Christ-Centered Spirituality Practice: Breath Prayer (Morning)

1. Dallas Willard, "Dallas' Personal Daily Practices?," interview, August 16, 2011, posted August 19, 2011, YouTube, 6 min., 3 sec., youtube.com/watch?v=GqLmeubS65Q.
2. Acts 13:22.

2.2: The Comparison Trap

1. This quote is often attributed to Theodore Roosevelt.

2.3: The Logical Flaw of Comparison

1. Genesis 1:10, 12, 18, 21, 25; see also 1:4, 31.
2. "Vocab Insight: Tov/Good," BibleProject, bibleproject.com /explore/video/vocab-insight-tov-good.
3. 1 Corinthians 8:1.

2.4: Atonement

1. 1 John 4:10–11.
2. Lexical Summary, s.v. "3725. *kippur,*" Bible Hub, biblehub. /hebrew/3725.htm.
3. Romans 6:23.
4. Leviticus 16:7–10.
5. Hebrews 7:27.
6. 2 Corinthians 5:21.
7. Matthew 11:28.

2.5: In Christ

1. Romans 5:8.

2.6: Gnosticism

1. Irenaeus, *Against Heresies,* preface to book 1, in *The Ante-Nicene Fathers: Translations of the Fathers down to A.D. 325,* ed. Alexander Roberts and James Donaldson, vol. 1, *The Apostolic Fathers, Justin Martyr, Irenaeus* (Charles Scribner's Sons, 1913), 315.
2. Stevan Davies, trans., *The Secret Book of John,* 2005, The Gnostic Secret Library, gnosis.org/naghamm/apocjn-davies.html.
3. Mark M. Mattison, trans., *The Gospel of Thomas,* Gospels.net, gospels.net/thomas.
4. "The Text of the Gospel of Thomas," from the Scholars Version translation published in *The Complete Gospels,* lifeintegrity.com /Gospel-of-Thomas-Scholars-Version.pdf.
5. Matthew 11:28.
6. J. Warner Wallace has a lot of great resources on his website to help you get started: coldcasechristianity.com/tag/gnostic-gospels.
7. Robert Barron, "The Genius of St. Irenaeus," YouTube, October 18, 2021, 35 min., 11 sec., youtube.com/watch?v=db_30gftdOo.
8. Matthew 16:25.
9. Mark 9:35.
10. Luke 9:23.

2.7: Manifesting

1. This quote was popularized by Joe Dispenza.
2. Mark 10:51.
3. Mark 10:51.
4. Mark 10:52.
5. Romans 12:2.
6. *The Secret,* directed by Drew Heriot (Prime Time Productions, 2006).
7. Luke 11:1–4.
8. "The Blessing," featuring Kari Jobe and Cody Carnes, track 4 on Elevation Worship, *Graves into Gardens,* Elevation Worship Records, 2020.

3.1: The Me-Maze (Part 3)

1. Timothy Keller, *The Freedom of Self-Forgetfulness: The Path to True Christian Joy* (10Publishing, 2012), 32.

3.2: The Old Self, the New Self, and the Problem with Self-Help

1. Acts 7:60.
2. Acts 9:4–5.
3. Acts 9:18.
4. Colossians 3:9–10.
5. Ephesians 4:22–24.
6. Romans 6:6–7.
7. 2 Corinthians 5:17.
8. Romans 7:19.
9. Romans 8:13.
10. One example is Philippians 1:22.
11. Genesis 1:31.
12. Steven R. Guthrie, *Creator Spirit: The Holy Spirit and the Art of Becoming Human* (Baker Academic, 2011), 63.
13. John H. Coe and Kyle C. Strobel, introduction to *Embracing Contemplation: Reclaiming a Christian Spiritual Practice,* ed. John H. Coe and Kyle C. Strobel (IVP Academic, 2019), 8.
14. This is from a helpful (and free) lecture series. John Coe teaches at Biola University. The course is called TTSF 501: Introduction to Spiritual Formation, and this point is from the lecture "Forming the Spirit."
15. Galatians 5:19–21.
16. To be clear, there's another problem with the self-help world. It often serves as an on-ramp to much darker spiritual practices. But here I'm using *self-help* to refer to those practices that we all agree

are great supplements for a healthy lifestyle but that so easily get twisted into the things that will save you.

17. John 16:7, ESV.

3.3: How the Helper Helps

1. Matthew 28:19–20.
2. Mark 6:37.
3. John 14:16, ESV.
4. John 14:26, ESV.
5. John 16:7, ESV.
6. Acts 2:4, ESV.
7. Gordon D. Fee, *God's Empowering Presence: The Holy Spirit in the Letters of Paul* (Baker Academic, 2009).
8. Acts 2:37.
9. Acts 2:42–47.
10. Steven R. Guthrie, *Creator Spirit: The Holy Spirit and the Art of Becoming Human* (Baker Academic, 2011), 122.
11. 1 Corinthians 12:3.
12. Guthrie, *Creator Spirit,* 122.
13. Philippians 2:7–8.
14. Mark 10:45.

3.5: Holy, Holy, Holy

1. Isaiah 6:3.
2. Isaiah 6:5.
3. *Major prophet* is just a fancy way of saying his book is one of the longer ones.
4. Isaiah 6:6–7.
5. Hebrews 12:28.
6. Ephesians 4:2.
7. Dallas Willard, "Truth: Can We Do Without It?," Dallas Willard Ministries, dwillard.org/resources/articles/truth-can-we-do-without-it.

3.7: Neither Puffed Up nor Deflated

1. Matthew 21:1–9.
2. Matthew 27:20–23.
3. Luke 3:21–22; 4:1.
4. Luke 22:24; John 13:4–5.
5. Ephesians 5:18.
6. Ephesians 3:17–19.
7. *Strong's Exhaustive Concordance*, s.v. "4137. *plēroó*," Bible Hub, biblehub.com/greek/4137.htm.

8. Romans 12:12, NLT.
9. Ephesians 4:31.
10. 2 Corinthians 12:9.

Christ-Centered Spirituality Practice: Meditation (Evening)

1. Matthew 11:28.
2. Psalm 1:1–2.
3. *Strong's Exhaustive Concordance,* s.v. "1897. *hagah,*" Bible Hub, biblehub.com/hebrew/1897.htm.

4.1: The Me-Maze (Part 4)

1. *Wall-E,* directed by Andrew Stanton (Pixar, 2008).

4.2: Revival

1. Matthew 11:28.

4.3: I Want You to Like ~~Me~~ (You)

1. Mark 12:31.
2. This quote is attributed to advice columnist Ann Landers, the pen name of Ruth Crowley and Esther Pauline Friedman.
3. Luke 9:23.

4.4: Psychedelics

1. Although ketamine isn't technically classified as a psychedelic, it can produce psychedelic-like experiences.
2. Luke 15:13.
3. Eugene H. Peterson, *A Long Obedience in the Same Direction: Discipleship in an Instant Society* (IVP, 2021), 9–10.
4. Friedrich Nietzsche, quoted in Peterson, *Long Obedience,* 11.
5. Peterson, *Long Obedience,* 10.
6. Peterson, *Long Obedience,* 11.

4.5: Astrology

1. Allyson Shaw, "Total Solar Eclipse," *National Geographic Kids,* 2025, kids.nationalgeographic.com/space/article/total-solar-eclipse.
2. Oxford Reference, s.v. "astrology," oxfordreference.com/display 10.1093/oi/authority.20110803095430709.
3. Erlend Gehlken, *Weather Omens of "Enūma Anu Enlil": Thunderstorms, Wind and Rain (Tablets 44–49)* (Brill, 2012), 5.
4. Daniel 2:10–11.
5. Daniel 2:12.
6. Daniel 2:27–28.
7. Matthew 2:1, ESV.
8. *Astrology Survey: The Role of Astrology in Society* (The Harris Poll

Thought Leadership Practice, February 2024), 2–3, theharrispoll.com/wp-content/uploads/2024/02/Astrology-Survey-February-2024.pdf.

9. Linda Rodriguez McRobbie, “How Are Horoscopes Still a Thing?,” *Smithsonian,* January 5, 2016, smithsonianmag.com/history/how-are-horoscopes-still-thing-180957701.
10. Aaron Earls, “Scripture Engaged: Who Are American Bible Readers?,” Lifeway Research, April 27, 2023, research.lifeway.com/2023/04/27/scripture-engaged-who-are-american-bible-readers.
11. “Astrology Market Expected to Reach $22.8 Billion by 2031,” Allied Market Research, alliedmarketresearch.com/press-release/astrology-market.html.
12. Psalm 19:1.
13. Psalm 8:3–4.

4.6: All the Known You Need

1. THINQ Media, “Is Fame All It’s Cracked Up to Be: Tony Hale,” YouTube, 3 sec., May 23, 2019, youtube.com/watch?v=WdwGllyABk0.
2. Galatians 6:2.

4.7: The Necessary Tension

1. Matt came across an article by Larry Osborne on crosswalk.com called “Is It a Sin to Be Average?” The article is an excerpt from Osborne’s book *A Contrarian’s Guide to Knowing God: Spirituality for the Rest of Us* (Multnomah, 2007).
2. Genesis 15:5.
3. Psalm 8:3–4.
4. Psalm 8:5–6.
5. Jeffrey Tacklind, *The Winding Path of Transformation: Finding Yourself Between Glory and Humility* (IVP Academic, 2019), 135.
6. Tacklind, *Winding Path,* 136.
7. Psalm 33:6–7. Although the text doesn’t tell us who wrote Psalm 33, lots of scholars attribute it to David.

About the Author

Ryan Wekenman is a storyteller and pastor who is passionate about finding creative ways to help people explore life's biggest questions. He is the author of *Single Today* and the co-host of two podcasts, *Stories in Scripture,* a show that brings the Bible to life for people all around the world, and *Afterthoughts,* a weekly conversation about faith, culture, and the church. He has a master's degree from Talbot School of Theology and is the teaching pastor of Red Rocks Austin, a young, vibrant church he helped start with a few of his best friends. He lives in Austin, Texas.